My Journey
My Journal

This Journal Is Inspired by
Trailblazing, Best-Selling Authors

Compiled by Viki Winterton

My Journey My Journal

©2018 by Viki Winterton

Expert Insights Publishing
1703 Sudderth Drive #352
Ruidoso, New Mexico 88345

Compiled by: Viki Winterton

Cover Design: Terry Z

Edited by: Pam Murphy

15 14 13 12 11 1 2 3 4 5

A portion of the profits from this book will be donated to Dolly Parton's Imagination Library – 1 million free books are mailed to children monthly. (https://imaginationlibrary.com)

"How wonderful it is that nobody need wait a single moment before starting to improve the world."
~ Anne Frank

Introduction
By Hal Price

"<u>A Heart's Journey Home</u>"

When you know yourself you can't be lost

And your life will take you far.

The key is being TRUE TO YOU

And remembering who you are.

Respect all life, it's here for you

And trust your heart to guide.

Know love surrounds you every day.

It never leaves your side.

Remember, every word and thought

Creates the world you'll see.

And say 'I Love You' every day....

And say it joyfully!

After serving as a lifetime marketing and branding executive for two Fortune 100 companies, his own branding agency and for professional athletes (including Four-Time NASCAR Champion, Jeff Gordon), Hal moved from Atlanta, GA in 2015 to the small beach town of Carpinteria, CA to put his heart and acquired skills to work writing and telling stories, volunteering and speaking.

In 2015, Hal begin using his creative, marketing and writing skills to fuel his passion for helping children. With his writing, Hal inspires children to discover their "soul's wisdom" and encourages them to use their unique gifts in the world.

He does this through his HEROIC HEART STORIES platform and he is launching the foundational series of books from this line called, "The Eli Bear Series" with Book One: *A Heart's Journey Home.*

Hal is currently completing a series of both Family Books as well as Children's books designed to teach key virtues and lessons of the heart from listening to the "secret whispers of their inner wisdom." www.elibearstories.com

"I was warned, 'You're not going to make money selling books. You're going to make money by having a book and using it to close more deals.' That has been my experience – an experience far exceeding my goals and my vision!

When you do what you love and you do it in the company of visionaries and household names, you become an instant expert in your field. You owe it to the world to get your story out in a book."

Viki Winterton, Publisher, #1 International Best-Selling Author, and Founder of Expert Insights Publishing. MyBookMyBiz.com

My Journey

— *DAY 1* —

My Journey

"The phrase, 'mental toughness' is very popular right now. To me, the mindset that is so important is one of self-compassion and self-nurturance. To be able to give our all, especially over the long term, requires an attitude towards oneself that is incredibly kind, compassionate, gentle, and nurturing. Treat yourself with true compassion and genuine self-care."

Sandra Joseph is a history-making Broadway Star turned inspirational Keynote Speaker and Best-Selling Author.
SandraJoseph.com

My Journey

— _DAY 2_ —

My Journey

"Most people want happiness, riches and significance which can become a reality when we use the enormous power and great treasures buried within us. Using these treasures wisely to realize your ideals, unleashes and expresses **Real Power** *which translates into achievement, fulfillment, influence and peace of mind. Realizing your ideals and maximizing your contributions to society enhances your success and significance. Your Ideal – like a polished diamond – brings out your brilliance, magnificence and worth."*

Dr. Princely Ebwe, Speaker, Educator, Author, Consultant, and Founder of Imperative Ideals, is devoted to expanding human awareness and empower people/organizations to realize their ideals, power and significance. <u>ImperativeIdeals.com</u>

My Journey

_____

_____

_____

_____

_____

_____

_____

_____

_____

_____

_____

_____

_____

My Journey

"What code do you live by? Does it consist of honesty, ethics, sincerity, honor, trustworthiness, fairness, authenticity and integrity? Sounds impossible, doesn't it? Absolutely not! Choosing to adhere to this code enables you to be YOU at your greatest good. Each night when you go to sleep, you'll have peace of mind that you gave your very best. In today's world, this code is more important than ever. Living by this code will ripple out, affecting many."

Pam Murphy is an entrepreneur who empowers her clients to create their ideal businesses by removing their obstacles blocking their way. pamurphy49@gmail.com

My Journey

— _DAY 4_ —

My Journey

— *DAY 5* —

"When you are thirsty, your body is telling you to drink. When you are hungry, your body is telling you to eat. When you are lonely, your body is telling you to eat. No! When you are lonely, your body is telling you to call a friend! Remember to not suffer in silence. Feel your feelings. Speak your truth. There is hope!"

John Crossman, husband, father of two girls and CEO of Crossman & Company. He is also the author of *CareerKillers/CareerBuilders.*   JCrossman@CrossmanCo.com

My Journey

— _DAY 5_ —

My Journey

"A good leader should be a mentor, and I've always tried to be that. I had mentors who helped me through my early years, giving me the experience necessary to proceed. I try to share that with the team members with whom I work. Bounce innovative ideas off of them, see what their reactions are, and then listen to what they are saying. I always respected the team members' ideas and their competence – they were very bright individuals. I listened to what they had to say."

Terry Zweifel, Aerospace Engineer, #1 Int'l Best-Selling Author, responsible for 23 patents for safe air travel.
TerryZweifel.com

My Journey

— _DAY 6_ —

My Journey

"Years after my 5-year cancer battle, I was asked to share one important message with the audience. Without thinking, I blurted out 'take five to save five!'

What most of us, including pre-cancer me, forget to do is to take time out...take five minutes to just breathe, smell flowers, feel sand under our feet, hug a tree, pet a dog, laugh out loud over nothing...and journal.

So stop everything right now and take five (minutes) to save five (years)!"

Dr. Marilyn Joyce, Award-Winning Speaker and Mentor, #1 International Best-Selling Author, Go-To Stress Release Expert & Creator of the Stress to Success Formula. TheStressToSuccessFormula.com

My Journey

_____

_____

_____

_____

_____

_____

_____

_____

_____

_____

_____

_____

_____

_____

My Journey

"I believe the fountain of youth is an internal state of being. When your life is balanced and you love what you are doing, the more youthful and alive your soul becomes. Beauty is truth; and the more truthful we are in our lives, the more beautiful we appear to others. When in balance, you can begin to manifest whatever you wish, including the fountain of youth, which is within you for you to discover."

Devin DeVasquez is a Best-Selling Author, Actress, Emmy Award Winning Producer, Model and Entrepreneur.
DevinDeVasquez.com

My Journey

— *<u>DAY 8</u>* —

My Journey

"When you reach out to others while you're writing for research, for their insights, even in email to ask a simple question, there are wonderful people who may be very busy, but when they recognize a sincere question in an area of expertise where they can lend a hand, they're are quick to support and assist. You'll be surprised how easy it is to extend yourself to include others in your work and build rich relationships."

Cathy Greenberg, PhD., is a *New York Times* Best-Selling Author, world-renowned Leadership Coach, Educator, Entrepreneur and Major Media Star. FearlessLeadersGroup.com

My Journey

— _DAY 9_ —

My Journey

"To create your best life, think of it like a garden. Your 'Garden of Life' will take careful planning and preparation. You will need to prepare the soil (create a state of mind that attracts powerful, positive experiences), decide what you want to grow or attract, and then deliberately put the right seeds in the earth. After that, your Garden will require continued love and care to ensure the best environment to attract and create what you envision."

Lorae Marsten, Law of Attraction Coach, Vedic Astrologer, Healer, Writer, works with people who crave more from life. She gives them tools to manifest a life of joy and abundance. BluePearlAstrology.com

My Journey

— _DAY 10_ —

My Journey

"The:

- ♦ *cock crowing the break of day;*
- ♦ *first bird tweeting the dawn chorus;*
- ♦ *sun rise in all its beauty;*
- ♦ *jewelled colours of kingfishers on the wing;*
- ♦ *first flowers of spring nuzzling through the snow;*
- ♦ *scents of summer flowers;*
- ♦ *drone of bees;*
- ♦ *discovery of shy newts in the garden pond.*

Being mindful, journaling natural things, ensures you have an unexpected richness to lift your spirits for all time."

Susie Briscoe is a Contributor to Life, Humanitarian, Int'l Business Executive Lifestyle Coach & Mentor, Master Leadership with Legacy Mentor; Contributing Author to 5 Int'l #1 books.   AcerCoachingAssociates.com

My Journey

— _DAY 11_ —

My Journey

"With any health or lifestyle issue, I look at the whole person. We are spiritual beings having a physical experience. So together we explore the mental, emotional and spiritual elements of the physical ailment. What is happening physically is the outer manifestation of what is going on internally. The body is an instrument of the mind."

Charlene Day, Your Wellness Mission Agent, is a Lifestyle and Leadership Coach, #1 International Best-Selling Author.
CharleneDay.com

My Journey

— _DAY 12_ —

My Journey

"A book is a book is a book ... unless it isn't. Magnificent writing sprouts up in all manner of genre – blogs, websites, short stories, letters to the editor, and even letters to friends. The key to producing a great book is to find the genre that best suits your personal style. You've been "writing" for years. Now let it fly!"

MaryAnn Shank, Web Pro for Solopreneurs. As a "niche" and "monetization" specialist, MaryAnn has inspired thousands of women. Over 30 publications. HerBizNow.com

My Journey

— _DAY 13_ —

My Journey

"The window for Coco's recovery was closing. The vet suggested hind-leg wheels, I wasn't ready to give up the fight or accept defeat. I prayed for guidance. My Divine download included a baby pram for walks and YouTube videos on canine physiotherapy. The window closed but Coco stood up and walked the night before my birthday.

It was a lesson in the Power of Prayer, asking and receiving Divine Support and taking action with Faith."

Vatsala Shukla, Career & Business Coach, Best-Selling Author and Change Catalyst mentors professionals to achieve their desired career aspirations and authentic life balance. KarmicallyCoaching.com

My Journey

— _DAY 14_ —

My Journey

"We could journey through life dancing, kissing existence into being, weaving love into patterns of spirit, touching each other's heart, remembering each other's soul, embracing, merging, being. Each moment is a moment of creation; each step leaves a footprint in the sand. What magic will you create by your very presence in the world? Let your heart be your guide on your journey through life."

Metka Lebar is a Best-Selling Author, Visionary and a Consciousness Facilitator who helps people activate their true potential. AccessOneness.com

My Journey

— <u>DAY 15</u> —

My Journey

"Emotions are powerful healing medicine. When you acknowledge and feel them, they actually leave you, layer by layer. There doesn't need to be a story or a drama attached, just ride the waves. Breathe and feel. Chances are, whatever you're feeling is something you originally experienced in childhood that you've been reminded of, re-evoking the same feelings. By being with the feelings, you forge new neural pathways, effectively re-wiring yourself in a very positive way."

Amrita Grace is a Visionary Priestess and Empowered Feminine Leader, Award-Winning, Best-Selling Author, Certified Spiritual Sexual Educator, and Co-Founder of The Sacred Feminine Mystery School. AmritaGrace.com

My Journey

My Journey

 *"Journaling has been an integral part of my life journey for more than 30 years. My personal reason for journaling was to consciously live a life I loved with intention through purposeful creation. By reaching for the joy in this moment right now, while being in a state of deep gratitude, I am opening myself up to life's limitless possibilities... and the many miracles manifesting in ways that I never imagined possible."*

Rita Koivunen is a #1 Int'l Best-Selling, Award-Winning Author, an Award-Winning & Published Artist, a Colour Therapist & Therapeutic Watercolour Workshop Facilitator. RitaKoivunen.com

My Journey

— _DAY 17_ —

My Journey

"Do you ever have days when the harder you juggle all the things on your plate, the easier it is to lose your balance and tumble? Being on the ground gives you a chance to actually look at things from a different perspective. A chance to look up. A moment to reevaluate your life and maybe even choose a different path. One to take you all the way to the stars and beyond!"

Donna L. Martin, Publisher at Story Catcher Publishing, Host of *Book Nook Reviews* & *Writerly Wisdom*, Member of SCBWI & CBI and Author of *LUNADAR: Homeward Bound*. StoryCatcherPublishing.com

My Journey

— _DAY 18_ —

My Journey

"Our very existence is to influence others through our experiences and transparency. Do not be defined by the World, be refined because of your exposure in the world. Become better and not bitter because of life's pitfalls. Influence is a road map to persuasion. Perplex minds should not be private but immersed in improving of one's self. Be the voice of reasoning which looks at fear as facing everything and releasing it."

Bridget C. Williams is an Entrepreneur and the Author of   Adjusting Your life Style Book Series. Since 2016, she has written 21 books, which are available on Barnes and Nobles/Amazon.
www.adjustingyourlifestyleandfrugalspending.wordpress.com

My Journey

— <u>*DAY 19*</u> —

My Journey

"Boundaries give you freedom. Good Boundaries: How long and how late you work. Always practicing Extreme Self-Care. Limiting what tasks you agree to do. Having time with family that you don't sacrifice.

At your funeral, no one will care about how you worked a lot or about that killer marketing launch. They will talk about how you were a loving parent, a mate who was always there. Have Boundaries. Keep to them. Set yourself free."

Kerry Mensior is The Audience Whisperer. He is also an Executive Speaking Coach and certified Master Instructor. Kerry loves "Teaching People How to Teach."
TheAudienceWhisperer.com

My Journey

— DAY 20 —

My Journey

"The most significant Aha is realizing that life doesn't happen 'To' you, it happens 'For' you. There's wisdom to be mined from every experience, whether windfall or wound. Asking: Truth: If X happened/is happening for my highest and best, what might that be? *provides personal choice regarding the gifts to extract from any experience. What if embracing this aware-ness is the missing element in being open to the infinite possibilities which are available to you?"*

Maureen Marie Damery, Self-Empowerment Facilitator, Author of the book/workshop, *Your Owner's Manual For Life~Source Code of Your Soul,* former Microsoft Software Engineer. MaureenDamery.com

My Journey

_____

_____

_____

_____

_____

_____

_____

_____

_____

_____

_____

_____

_____

— _DAY 21_ —

My Journey

"One day our journey shall come to pass. As we look back at our life, we may have regrets, sadness, happiness and pure delight. This rich journey is ever evolving. From birth to death, from body to soul. Allow your essence to fuel a fire so bright that your journey becomes one of passion and purpose...full of so much fire and desire you shall shine forevermore...even after your journey here has ended, remember there is no end to YOU."

Jaz Gill is a poet and lyricist. Author of *True Grace* and the single hit, "Preach", Jaz hopes to promote healing through the written word.   JazGill.com

My Journey

My Journey

"'What I feel + what I think = what I do and how I see myself.' If I feel and think I am crap, then everything I do is crap and I am crap. The longer I live crap, the harder it is to get out of the crap. What would your life be like if you started each day looking for the good you do and encouraging others to have a great day?"

David Lawson is a Relationships Coach Helping YOU to LIVE a Better Life through Stronger & Healthier Relationships - Personally & Professionally!   FindingtheLight.com.au

My Journey

— *DAY 23* —

My Journey

"After being kicked out the church from burnout and mental health challenges, it felt like I was sleep walking for many years. I was stuck in feelings of abandonment, betrayal, anger and regret. Once I embraced the reality that I needed to do some inner work and heal, things began to shift. You have to kick fear and shame to the curb, do your inner work and walk in the authority you already have within."

Alicia Buchanan is the Author of "From Exile to EMBRACE" Series, Texas Licensed Clinical Social Worker, Transformational Speaker, Wellness/Life Connoisseur and former Brand Ambassador for *Oprah* Magazine.   AliciaBuchanan.com

My Journey

— _DAY 24_ —

My Journey

"Love is a verb. There are so many kinds of love: for every person, blessing, gift, experience and circumstance. Some loves are instinctual, some are choices. Some are really hard work. Enemies, ordeals, trials – these ask more of us than all the others. That is why they are there. Character for the soul, golden imprints on the spirit. It took me decades to learn this. I deeply wish you easier lessons and gentler teachers."

Ursula Nieuwoudt from Namibia, SW Africa, Int'l Best-Selling Co-Author and Author of _Practical Conversations About Fitting In_. She is working on her next book about diamonds. UrsulaNieuwoudt.com

My Journey

— _DAY 25_ —

My Journey

"I thought I had to hide this 'curse' of being able to see, feel and hear people's as well as animals' thoughts and emotions. I thought 'Why did I have this burden to bear?' Then I realized I could use my talents to heal then release victims from their suffering.

By changing my perspective on my talent, I changed my life. Try to see all sides of a situation. Look for the good in everything life brings you."

Mary Carol Ross, Life Strategist, Medical Intuitive, Speaker, Medium, Spiritual Healer, Mediator, Master Intuitive and Author of many spiritual books, including *Ally's Spiritual Journey*.   MaryCarolRoss.com

My Journey

— <u>DAY 26</u> —

My Journey

"While it is true that genealogy is the study of one's ancestors, it's often more than just seeking a few names and dates. Genealogy affords an opportunity to delve into the depths of your genetic content and connect to those who share that same genetic code.

It offers you a sense of belonging and a glimpse of where you fit in the grand scheme of the universe. So get searching and uncover those roots!"

Shawnese Sullivan, proofreader and editor, founder of Uradel Publishing, genealogy writer, and creator of The Kin Cottage.   UradelPublishing@gmail.com

My Journey

— _DAY 27_ —

My Journey

— *DAY 28* —

*"Paying all your life for what was done to you when too young to defend yourself against it, is debilitating, distorted and extinct. Exact revenge: Rebel-love **yourself.***

*Let love be a genuine deal without artifice or sacrifice and **not** a dysfunctional, hot pursuit, born out of an unrequited, neurotic need for validation to be seen and adored. Watch others respond beautifully to your honesty, your brave, transparent leaning and the rest falls into place."*

Pam Wood is a Body Mind Coach. 'How To Have A Happy Childhood At Last!', the extraordinary result of her 'Transform Your Life' Program.   TheGardenofDivineElements.co.uk

My Journey

My Journey

"Discover your essence to contribute to the world your unique energy signature. When I truly understood my authentic self and was willing to accept the responsibility of being in my own authority, I was in right relationship with myself and the earth and the possibilities were endless.

Shine your vibrant light to be the catalyst for change. The journey within empowers you to be influential with the ability to respond from the heart."

Discover Your Essence with **Wanda Davis, M.Sc., B.Sc., B.Ed.,** who is a Certified Coach/Energy Conductor, member of Canadian Association of Professional Speakers and Best-Selling Author.   WandaDavis.ca

My Journey

— _DAY 29_ —

My Journey

"I was floating in outer space, marveling at the beauty and serenity of the Universe. Nothing but Love and Joy filled me. Deep in meditation I KNEW that we are eternal beings in an irrelevant mortal shell. 'Yes, but your shell is a gift. Take care of it!'

The message was crystal clear. The next day I made my overdue dermatology appointment where I was diagnosed with cancer, just in time.

NEVER doubt your intuition!"

Dr. Irena Kay, Relationship Success Coach, retired Gynecologist, Marriage Facilitator, developed techniques that integrate mind and brain work to help couples overcome the love divide.   MarriedLoveSuccess.com

My Journey

— _DAY 30_ —

My Journey

"You have a divine purpose in this lifetime. Your insight, experiences, successes and failures, beliefs and values are uniquely yours and your journey so far has led to this very moment. Our world needs happiness, kindness, nurturing, sustainable solutions, community connectedness, and peace.

You can help just by being you! Align with your calling. What brings you joy? What makes your heart sing and your soul soar? What will be your gift to our world?"

Fiona-Louise is a Natural Therapist, Author, Educator, and Video Creator for soulful businesses. Discover her best-selling book collaborations, musings & more.   Fiona-Louise.com

My Journey

— _DAY 31_ —

My Journey

"I was in the audience of a huge internet marketing conference and realized, 'If I'm going to be as successful as the people up on stage, I need to make decisions that scare me and take action anyway.'

So that's what I did. Twelve months later, I had launched a new business, replaced my previous year's income and I was the speaker up on that stage.

Embrace feeling 'scarecited'. That's where the magic happens."

Janet Beckers, #1 International Best-Selling Author, Multi-Award Winning Online Marketing Strategist, Speaker, and Mentor known for making the complex simple with a healthy dose of reality and humor.   RomanceYourTribe.com

My Journey

My Journey

" 'You're not a singer!'

The words stung sharply.

My life was being swept under the carpet, squashed down by one who mattered.

Wrong! Wrong! Wrong!

I am a singer, a writer, a dramatist, a Creative – but unfortunately, you don't like my song. Unfortunately, my life is not being lived to your liking.

You can't please everyone. Be who you were created to be. Don't lose the essence of who you are. Lift your heart-song.

Sing!"

Pat Moore BA (Hons) Theatre Arts, PGCE, a teacher for 30 years, Pat is passionate about creative ministry. Co-writer of Salvation belongs to our God. Release the Arts in you. Praisepen.uk

My Journey

_____

_____

_____

_____

_____

_____

_____

_____

_____

_____

_____

_____

— _DAY 33_ —

My Journey

"Do you seek Greater Success? Greater Health? Peak Performance in sports and business? A higher sense of well-being? How about a faster recovery from surgery?

Practicing Gratitude will give you all that and more! When we practice giving thanks for all we have, we give ourselves the chance to see all of life as an opportunity and a blessing. It's a matter of where we put our focus and attention. What are you grateful for?"

Dr. Inessa Zaleski, Int'l Speaker, Hypnotherapist, Creator of Reikinosis®, helps successful individuals gain laser focus and embody pleasure in order to increase joy, success and influence! <u>Calmness.com</u>

My Journey

My Journey

"Fashion has always helped me accomplish great things despite being bullied and having very low self-esteem as a young child. When I started school, I got so much recognition because of the way I dressed. It increased my confidence instantly. My vision is for all of us to embrace our unique essence and personal style and claim our power by feeling great about how we dress. From experience, it's the easiest and quickest way to radiate authentic confidence."

Josee Brisebois (pronounced Jo-Zay Breeze-bwa), Personal Style Expert for Women Leaders, Speakers & Entrepreneurs, and Founder of "Unleash Your Unique Wow Factor" style transformation course.   WeCanStyle.com

My Journey

— <u>DAY 35</u> —

My Journey

"It's so important to get out there and do the work you are meant to do in the world! When those voices come up in your head saying 'You can't do this!' or 'You're not qualified to fulfill your life purpose!', know that it's your ego (lower energy) trying to pull you off your path. When these voices come up, it actually means that you're on the right path, so take heart!"

Cornelia Ward is a Divine Career and Business Coach who helps lightworkers create a career or business that really lights them up!   IHelpPeopleLoveMondays.com

My Journey

— _DAY 36_ —

My Journey

"Mastering the human factor in leadership is a prerequisite to get the right things done and skyrocket team performance. That's what successful high performing leaders do. It's all about how you connect and communicate, coax and coach, secure collaboration and commitment.

Whether you take the lead in business, community, or family affairs, at the end of the day it's the people involved and their environment that matter. They define your level of success or failure!"

John A. Williams, MSc, AKA 'The Pragmaticioner', Business Consultant, #1 Best-Selling Author, and Developer of the people-centered Pragmatic Leadership Formula™. JAWConsultancy.com

My Journey

My Journey

"Real charity helps people to help themselves and gain self-esteem. We should seek to understand the needs of the poor and needy and provide the help that will benefit them the most. Food, laundry, transportation, and a shower are usually the basic necessities. The truest charity is when you sacrifice your resources to help another person. To give of your self, time, effort, and friendship, costs far more than a simple handout."

Lorraine Price is a book coach, author, book reviewer, proofreader, and copywriter focused on non-fiction storytelling.   Lprice9559@gmail.com

My Journey

My Journey

"My vision for the world is to create Sustainable Generational Change. The only way this is going to happen is by knowing that every single element of our world is being taken care of: the earth, the plants, the animals, the people, the water, the community projects, and the visions and dreams of the children. I have never given up on this dream and I never will. I am one hundred percent committed to my vision."

Stacey Huish is Founding Director of 1000 Ripple Effects, a Speaker, Author, Earth Healer, Heart Healer, powerful Game Changer and Lover of Life!   1000RippleEffects.com

My Journey

— *DAY 39* —

My Journey

"Within a 6-month period, I fled an abusive marriage, was laid off by a 'mini-Enron', and was diagnosed with breast cancer. I asked God, 'What now?' Immediately I heard, 'Draw closer to Me.' I consider that time all blessings.

God opened Hollywood doors to acting in film/TV. Little did I know He would literally push me into producing. When you keep your eyes focused on God, hang on to your hat for a wild ride!"

Susan Shearer, Actor, Award-Winning Film Producer, Writer, Director, Mentor and CEO of I'm Not A Turkey Productions.   ImNotATurkey.com

My Journey

— _DAY 40_ —

My Journey

"Your past mistakes do not define your future dreams, hopes and desires. You have gifts and talents hidden inside of you! Your destiny is calling out to you saying, 'Try hard and do not give up.' Life has a way of choking out our dreams, burying our hopes and visions under discouragement, past mistakes, failure, divorce, lack of support and encouragement from family or friends. Reignite the flame inside your heart... Your destiny is calling you!"

Rebecca M. Huey is an Entrepreneur, Ambassador to Akure, Ondo State, Nigeria, Africa and Founder of Cursive Kidz™, a Trademark of Education Creation LLC.   Cursive-Kidz.com

My Journey

— _DAY 41_ —

My Journey

— DAY 42 —

"When someone says you can't have it all, they are merely reflecting the limiting belief they have about themselves. Ignore statements like this and dream big and go for whatever you want. Every one of us has heard those 'words of wisdom' but they are not true unless you believe they are. So for 'money is the root of all evil' and 'you can't have it all,' simply CHOOSE to disagree and GO FOR IT."

Tracy Repchuk, 7 Time International Best-Selling Author, has spoken in 37 countries, 22 Major TV networks appearances, Forbes Coach, LinkedIn Influencer, Amazon Influencer, awards from President Obama and White House.
FastActionResults.com

My Journey

— *DAY 42* —

My Journey

— DAY 43 —

"Drinking half your weight in ounces is one of the best things you can do for your health. It clears up brain fog, mild headaches, makes your skin feel soft and supple, keeps your bowel movements regular and removes daily toxins from your body.

Start your day with a glass of room temperature water and then continue to drink throughout the day. Drink through a non-plastic straw to increase the amount in each sip!"

Chef Pamela Roberts, Host of *Charlotte Cooks*/ PBS Charlotte, Author of *Healthy & Hydrated – The Key to Vibrant Living*, Health Coach, Certified Chef promoting Healthy Cooking & Lifestyles ChefPamela.com

My Journey

My Journey

" 'It's a long, long road / From which there is no return' (Scott B., Russell B. "He Ain't Heavy, He's My Brother.")

Since life is finite and time keeps moving forward, you owe it to yourself to travel a path that is true to your heart. Do so by: Following your dreams. Celebrating yourself. Being your own best friend. Loving with all your heart. Living fully in each moment. And never giving up on achieving all your heart's desires."

Karen Fitts Penaluna is an international best-selling, inspirational author, and a transformational relationship coach guiding her clients to opening their hearts to finding everlasting Love!   KarenFittsPenaluna.com

My Journey

_____

_____

_____

_____

_____

_____

_____

_____

_____

_____

_____

_____

_____

_____

— <u>DAY 44</u> —

My Journey

"During my life, I have been tested with many challenges especially when it has come to relationships. Starting my first job, I found that people I encountered were not like my friends in school, could not be trusted, and would take advantage of me. I was hurt but I learned to never give up at love, trust, respect and helping others because these are the only forces from the Universe that can heal us and the Earth."

Carmen Apostoiu is a Construction Engineer, Entrepreneur in the personal development field and small business owner.   Carmina24.wordpress.com

My Journey

— DAY 45 —

My Journey

"Simple things make dreams come true. Are you looking for fulfillment and success in your own life? The key is to find a way to help others. The more you help others the closer you get to your goal. Help them get a better health, make new friends, financial security, travel the world or stay at home. We build surplus and inner wealth by helping others. You can start by being generous with a smile."

Jette Bilberg Lauritsen is a 3 time #1 International Best-Selling Author and a Health & Wellness Coach. Jettebl.MyASEAlive.com

My Journey

— _DAY 46_ —

My Journey

"Never let anyone tell you that you cannot heal!! I have now witnessed hundreds of my clients and patients heal from stuck medical and emotional issues. By tapping into your inner wisdom and letting it lead you exactly where you are required to be at any moment, you will discover ALL of the resources you need to heal your life!"

Markyia Nichols, MD aka Dr.Kyia, Board-Certified Physician and Functional Medicine Expert, author, empowerment guru and lover of yoga, energy healing, animals and nature. DrKyia.com

My Journey

_____

_____

_____

_____

_____

_____

_____

_____

_____

_____

_____

_____

_____

_____

— _DAY 47_ —

My Journey

"I was told you cannot do this alone; you need a team to help get your vision realized. So true, yet the first step is to have a clear vision, as it's the vision that attracts the team. We all have dreams sometime in our lives. Visualize your dream, and take action, because even initially going in the wrong direction will eventually take you in the right direction to make your dream a reality."

Sharón Lynn Wyeth, Professional Name Analyst, Radio Host, Speaker, and Best-Selling Author, Creator and Founder of Neimology® Science.   <u>KnowTheName.com</u>

My Journey

_____

_____

_____

_____

_____

_____

_____

_____

_____

_____

_____

_____

_____

_____

_____

— <u>DAY 48</u> —

My Journey

"Life gives you lots of opportunities to change miseries into happiness, but we miss them. That was my life until I couldn't survive anymore.

I chose to surrender my life to the highest power of us all.

It is the beginning of a powerful change with ups and downs but with peace and tranquility in life. I wanted to be free and it did so swiftly.

Life and wishes surrendered bring powerful and peaceful changes."

Kirtti S is an a Energy Alchemist and Coach, Founder and Director of SpiritualCuratives.com, Certified Reiki Master & Teacher and NLP Practitioner.   SpiritualCuratives.com

My Journey

— _DAY 49_ —

My Journey

— *DAY 50* —

"Want to live your best life? Ask questions, dig deeper, peel the onion! Most often, the best parts of life aren't easily attainable or visible. They're hiding under the surface. When you begin to ask more and learn more about yourself and others, you'll find things of great value. Learn more about yourself and those around you; you won't regret it. Curiosity didn't kill the cat; it let it out of the bag to go do great things!"

Tamica Sears is a Leadership Development Coach currently living in Arizona. She has also authored her new book, *You Are Enough*, available on Amazon. SearsCoaching.com

My Journey

— *DAY 50* —

My Journey

"At all times, myriads of angels surround us providing Divine Guidance along each step of our journey, dropping clues throughout each day, guiding us toward our Divine Purpose. We can stride confidently knowing our Angels have our back. Nothing is too small or too great; they are eager to help if but only asked. All we need do is stop and open our hearts to hear their messages of love and encouragement."

Teresa Christian has been a Life Purpose Coach for eleven years and is both a certified Angel Card Reader and Passion Test Facilitator.   TheAngelElement@gmail.com

My Journey

— _DAY 51_ —

My Journey

"Never give up on your dreams! Sometimes the timing is wrong. Revisit them occasionally. That visit may reveal that it's the perfect time to birth one of them.

Dormant since a high school senior, my writing dream materialized when I was 57. Now I'm living my dream retirement as a published author."

Joyce Ermeling Heiser is an Author, Speaker, Retirement Coach, *Chicken Soup for the Soul* Author, and co-founder Lighthouse Christian Writers.   JoyceHeiser.com

My Journey

— _DAY 52_ —

My Journey

"Powerful steps to empower any change:
• *You Choose – a desired outcome.*
• *You Let Go – of any resistance.*
• *You Take Action – on what you already know.*

The common element is YOU. There is nothing to get, learn, or do. You are enough! Just as you are - right now. You deserve your desires. Imagineer your journey – write now!

I deserve to ... I release ... How can I make this a reality?"

Leslie Atkinson, Soulful Adventurer, Catalyst for Peace and Understanding between peoples, Steward of public land and clean water. Founder of Leslie Atkinson Inc., Dirty Her, Reflex Racing, and Universal Solutions. LeslieAtkinson.com

My Journey

My Journey

"The greatest strength you will ever have is in embodying your personal truth because even when you're living from an empowered place, unanticipated challenges still happen from time to time that may be upsetting, disruptive, or scary.

Becoming — then staying — empowered means tuning in to your own internal compass, and trusting what's inside and acting from that place of trust. This will provide the strength necessary to face unanticipated challenges — and create the most personal satisfaction."

Kelly Lydick is an Author, Gateway Dreaming™ Coach, and founder of *Waking the Dream,* a boutique consulting firm offering creative writing and personal growth workshops, and private consultations.   KellyLydick.com

My Journey

— _DAY 54_ —

My Journey

"What are you looking to create in your life?

Did you know: What you think about, you talk about? And what you talk about, you bring about. You are the one who created your life; you are also the one who can un-create it.

Being honest with yourself, do you have more thoughts of abundance or lack? If you change your thoughts, you can change your life! What if NOW is your time to shine?!"

Susan Shatzer, 8 time #1 International Best-Selling Author, Energetic Success Coach, and Host of the TV Show, *Unlocking Your Limitless Life with Susan Shatzer.* SusanShatzer.com

My Journey

— <u>DAY 55</u> —

My Journey

"Your greatest breakthroughs and trans-formations will manifest as a result of developing self-awareness.

The more you know about your strengths, weaknesses, beliefs, behaviors, emotions, attitudes, motivations and even how others perceive you, the better equipped you'll be to learn something valuable from even the worst mistakes and most difficult of times.

Having self-awareness is empowerment — being deeply honest with yourself and being in control of your thoughts and emo-tions, not the other way around."

Jessica Brown, Personal Growth & Law of Attraction Blogger, online Entrepreneur, Champion for animal rights and mental health, Wife, Friend, Traveler, and Founder of manifesteveryday.com

My Journey

— _DAY 56_ —

My Journey

"Growing up I knew I was different/ unique born leader and sometimes I yearned to fit into a world where people tried to fit in. But I wasn't and no one really is. We live in a world where we are all different. No two people are alike. Instead of being like others, embrace who you are and the gifts you can give to the world. Know, shout out and embrace that being different is fun!"

Andrew Mondia is The Intuitive Traveler, an actor and speaker. AndrewMondia.com

My Journey

My Journey

"Write on the right-hand page of the journal first, leaving the left-hand page blank. Later, at specific intervals, review what you wrote. Then on the blank left-hand page, write what's changed. Compare what was happening to what's happening now — what changed? What will I do differently next time? What will I keep doing? Reviewing the past and answering questions like these allow me to understand my habits, beliefs and most importantly patterns of behaviors."

Sharon Sayler, Communications and Body Language Expert affectionately dubbed "the difficult people whisperer," #1 Int'l Best-Selling Author, and Int'l Trainer, teaching professionals to be courageous leaders.   SharonSayler.com/Gift/

My Journey

_____

_____

_____

_____

_____

_____

_____

_____

_____

_____

_____

_____

_____

— _DAY 58_ —

My Journey

"I love startups. ~ Taking an idea and vision to reality, through to fruition. ~ To be clear!

My journey has had many ups, downs, challenges and obstacles. Even once success is reached, shifts in economics, markets and politics have affected my journey.

The power of my mindset has been critical to my ability to achieve and sustain success. This is the path of every true successful entrepreneur and author."

"The Journey is the reward!"

Phil Ross is CEO of Enerintel and MDG International, a Best - Selling Author, and Producer of Soul Destiny Transformation books, workshops and Video series.
MasteryDevelopmentGroup.com

My Journey

— _DAY 59_ —

My Journey

"Is your comfort zone killing your dreams? Does fear have you hiding within your comfort zone? Get out of this trap! Push toward your dreams! They are a part of your calling, your journey in life. So, I challenge you: What are your dreams? What is one baby step that you can take today to move out of your comfort zone and toward your dreams? Take the challenge. Don't let your comfort zone control you."

Carma Spence, an Award-Winning Speaker, International Best-Selling Author, can help you unleash your inner Public Speaking Superhero and communicate your message with confidence.   PublicSpeakingSuperPowers.com

My Journey

My Journey

"Stress. What does it mean to you? Pressure; your job; the kids; or some big hairy guys waving spears at lions? Think again. Those are sources of stress. Stress itself is a mind-body response to situations and thoughts. Everyone has their own unique stress signature. To find yours, first, identify your sources of stress, and then identify how you usually respond - that is your unique stress signature. And you get to decide what that looks like."

Edna Brinkley, **PhD**, Licensed Psychologist, Women's Success Strategist, Author, International Speaker, and Trainer, helps professional women break free of their stress-worry cycle.   BrinkleyCenter.com

My Journey

My Journey

"I have been following the words and inspiration of several leaders and coaches for the past decade. I began to realize that most of them were very passionate about getting up very early in the morning and performing a daily routine before starting with the usual obligations. I wondered what could be so important about a daily routine and dismissed it. Until one day I tried. Now I cannot live without it!"

Sally Bendersky, Author, Coach, Engineer, Founder of New Leadership. She has transformed lives and leadership of hundreds of people while also leading as ambassador, Secretary of Higher Education, and on Boards.   SallyBCoach.com

My Journey

My Journey

"Have you ever heard the term, 'It's nothing personal...it's just business'? I have. And every time I do, it still disappoints me. Because today, business is personal. People do business with me because of me. And people should do business with you because of you. Not because you perfected some slick sales presentation or created an amazingly flashy website. Ask yourself this, 'What can I do today that proves that I value my professional relationships?'"

TR Garland, Wall Street Journal® Award Winner in Business, #1 Best-Selling Author of *Building The Ultimate Network*, Speaker, and Coaching Industry Veteran and Insider. TR@TRGarland.com

My Journey

_____

_____

_____

_____

_____

_____

_____

_____

_____

_____

_____

_____

_____

_____

_____

My Journey

"Adolescent notes were sporadically jotted in books secured with tiny locks designed to keep my brothers from peeking. Weeks could pass as blank pages, until, usually compelled by teen angst, I'd return to write. That diary became my best friend.

Diapers eventually replaced diaries; the friendship was shelved ... until major life changes led me to re-kindle that friendship. Since then, I've depended on daily journaling for clarity, wisdom and guidance. Commit to daily journaling! It's life-enhancing!"

Jan Deelstra, CEO of Winged-Women™ Business & Life Coaching, award-winning Author, uses her passion for writing to inspire women to emerge into their fullest potential. JanDeelstra.com

My Journey

— _DAY 64_ —

My Journey

"Yoga is 'The Ultimate Solution' for all problems in the world. How? All problems are human creation and Yoga is the science of refining humans. Yoga creates leaders of the highest order with power to change the world. Practice Yoga in its authentic and purest form, elevate humanity and end suffering. Yoga encompasses several techniques. Let's stop imprisoning Yoga by chaining it to mere fitness exercises. 'Liberate Yoga! Liberate You! Liberate the World!' Will you?"

Shanthi Yogini, Yoga Liberator, Yoga-Teacher Trainer of Lifestyle-Based Yoga, #1 Int'l Best-Selling Author, Speaker, and Founder of Yoga for Happiness Academy.
YogaForHappiness.com

My Journey

— <u>DAY 65</u> —

My Journey

"Envision where you want to be, really feel your dream. Then look at where you are right now, your starting point, and begin visualizing the road from here to your end goal. Let the steps you need to take emerge and bring them into the physical plane by buckling down and doing what it takes to make your dreams come true.

Trust in your vision, trust in your dream and not least: trust in yourself."

Merise McDowall, Founder of The Crystal School in Denmark, Journalist, and Author. She helps people find their inner true self and also educates crystal healers and therapists. Merise-McDowall.com

My Journey

— <u>DAY 66</u> —

My Journey

— _DAY 67_ —

"Ways to Brighten Your Day for Today, Tomorrow and Forever!

» *Imagine yourself like a sun that can turn a drab day into gold.*

» *Smile for no reason.*

» *Even in stillness, you can dance. You can dance to the silence of a random moment. The music of being alive. Of being part of the orchestral celebration of this day."*

Tantra Bensko, gold-medal-winning novelist, teaches fiction writing and edits manuscripts. Contact her and say hello! FlameFlower@runbox.com

My Journey

My Journey

"You are a unique and powerful creator. That is what makes you so special and amazing. Your hardships are what have formed you and given you your unique talents and abilities. Your challenges in life are what make you stronger. They are like the refiner's fire that heats at such a high temperature that impurities come to the surface and separate out, thus making you better. You are truly amazing and the world needs you!"

Joyce Blue is an empowerment coach who shows people how to set aside self-esteem and other struggles to live and lead lives they love.　joyce@EmpoweringYouLEC.com

My Journey

_____

_____

_____

_____

_____

_____

_____

_____

_____

_____

_____

_____

_____

_____

_____

_____

_____

My Journey

— _DAY 69_ —

"I've learned that Mindset isn't something. It's everything. This realization created an enormous shift in my life. All of a sudden a simple question like 'how are you' became an opportunity for me to make, what became, powerful life-changing mindset shifting decisions. An answer like 'I'm Amazing' created a new space for me to step into. Remember and know, we are always at choice; our life is a series of masterful, wise and powerful decisions."

Frank White MBA, PhD, Business & Executive Leadership Coach, Forum Certified Master Coach/Trainer, International Speaker, Success Coach and Personal Development Guru, nationally acclaimed speaker, management consultant and motivational expert. FrankWhiteInternational.com

My Journey

My Journey

— _DAY 70_ —

"Mindfulness — Breathing mindfully is the activity of paying attention to the breath as it moves in and out. Feeling the rise and fall of the chest and the belly. Noticing how the air flows around in the throat. Appreciating this life-giving system of lungs, diaphragm, trachea, mouth and nasal passages as the air enters and leaves your body. Sustaining every part with the energies of creation. This is your point of power. Choose wisely now."

Deena Efferson, Ceremony Director for Spiritual Unity Movement, Developer of the concert series, "Love Train", and she has extensive skills/expertise in creativity, healing and spirituality.   SpiritualUnityMovement.org

My Journey

— _DAY 70_ —

My Journey

"Tell your story. A story that can only be told by you. Make it personable. Write it in your own 'voice.' Don't try to polish it to be more 'sophisticated.' Just be you. You have a story that needs to be told. Writing has allowed me to share my experiences. It has opened doors for me to share my story – and get paid in the process. You can do the same. Write YOUR STORY!"

Robert Thibodeau, Author, Public Speaker, Founder and Host of the #1 rated online "Evangelism Radio" Christian radio station, "Kingdom Cross Roads Podcast." BobThibodeau.com

My Journey

— _DAY 71_ —

My Journey

"For a happy and successful life, you must continue to educate yourself. Knowledge is the key to success and can open many new opportunities. Nature's principle is growth or decay. You can either continue learning or become stagnant and stuck. Warren Buffet spends 80% of his time in reading and learning new skills. It's not a secret. To succeed and make your dreams come true, learn new skills to excel in today's fast changing world."

Khalid Yusuf Khan is an Analyst, Engineer, Blogger and Author of *Learn to Live Together* for helping families and newly married couples learn to get along.
BlogTechAnalysis@gmail.com

My Journey

— *DAY 72* —

My Journey

"What's stopping you from being YOU? COMPLEX PTSD? Do you feel misunderstood; can't see the light at the end of the tunnel? I know the struggle first hand. Those who judge and invalidate you don't know your struggle.

You are courageous, just to be surviving! Well, it is no longer a LIFE SENTENCE! With help, you can now embrace your storms and find hope again. It's TIME to discover the authentic YOU!"

Margaret Reece, **BA HONS,** on-line Mentor, Int'l Speaker, and Author of the forthcoming book *Hope Restored, a guide to embracing the storms of Complex PTSD.*
Margaret.Reece@btinternet.com

My Journey

My Journey

*"Suffering from device distraction disorder, stress, or overwhelm? If any of these describe you, then it is time for a little **YOU time** to cure your Nature Deficit Disorder. How? Escape into nature - like Idaho!   Enjoy stunning beauty, solitude, majestic mountains, placid pools and immense lakes and lay under the peaceful 360 degrees of silent darkness with the only light from star-filled skies above. You will feel more connected with Nature, focused, calm, content and grounded."*

As a Master Naturalist and Master Gardener, **Larry Meyer** lives a life he loves as an outdoorsman, an avid fisherman and an extensive Idaho traveler.   TheHeArtofLiving@aol.com

My Journey

— _DAY 74_ —

My Journey

"Working a decade in the medical field, I knew much about disease and little about health. Health, after all, is the absence of disease. My quest to discover true health and how to achieve it bore fruit. You are what you eat, digest, absorb and assimilate into every cell. You are what you think about, dwell upon and sound down into your heart. Nourish yourself physically, mentally, emotionally, and spiritually. Nourish; you flourish. Don't; you won't!"

Susanne Morrone, Speaker, Natural Health Consultant, Coach, Co-Author of a #1 Int'l Best-Selling Book, and Author. NaturalHealthChat.com

My Journey

My Journey

— _DAY 76_ —

"When we feel like we have a long way to go, we tend to procrastinate. Refer to your dreams and goals in the present tense so it no longer feels like a far-off idea. For example, say I 'have' a best-selling book instead of I 'will' have a best-selling book. Start to see your dreams in the present tense (in faith) and you will be ignited to launch forward towards them!"

Yentl Lega guides heart-working women towards feeling the way they want to feel and deserve to feel by reducing stress to maximize health.   <u>YOUnfolded.com</u>

My Journey

— _DAY 76_ —

My Journey

"Most of us are on a non-stop search for love and approval from others. At the same time, we're our own worst enemy, saying things to ourselves that we would never say to a friend.

It's time to stop fighting with yourself. Simply say one kind thing to yourself every day. Love yourself. Treat yourself as your best friend. You will magically find that when you treat yourself better, everyone else will too."

Jonathan Troen is Chief Life Officer, Founder of Austin Yoga Tree and the Life Mastery Collective, and Creator of the Self Love Revolution Masterclass, creating success through Love.   Troen.net

My Journey

My Journey

"There are many lessons of self-care and we often don't follow them. It is important to put yourself first because if you break down, you won't be strong enough for those around you.

When our emotions get the best of us, we fall apart. But when we take time for ourselves, things fall into place and our worries fade away.

It is time to think about yourself and get in some great 'me' time."

Catherine M. Laub, ACM, is a Turquoise Angel Guide, a 13-Time Award-Winning Author, Host of *The Celestial Spoon* Podcast, Mental Illness Advocate, Psychic/Medium and Spiritual Guide. CatherineMLaub.com

My Journey

_____

_____

_____

_____

_____

_____

_____

_____

_____

_____

_____

_____

_____

My Journey

"Life's an adventure that takes place with each moment we feel, with each idea we have, with each step we take. It depends on us to continue on the right track, full of energy and with a positive mindset. May your trails lead you in the right direction, making sure you're happy at every turn. Now, dare to take that step so the road ahead is on the course of success that you have set for yourself."

Luis Vicente Garcia is an International Best-Selling Author, award-winning Speaker, certified Business Performance Coach and member of the Bestselling Authors International Organization. @LVGarciaG

My Journey

_____

_____

_____

_____

_____

_____

_____

_____

_____

_____

_____

_____

_____

_____

— _DAY 79_ —

My Journey

"Only you control your destiny. Your thoughts, actions, and efforts are the result of who you are today or who you will become tomorrow. Create a vision so clear you can imagine every detail of it coming alive in your life. You are uniquely made and the only person in the universe with your fingerprints; a simple reminder you should make no comparisons. Your journey is yours to imagine, create, live and believe in."

Michelle Hammons, Certified High Performance Coach™, Coach, Speaker and Creative Artist, will help you look through the lens of your own life and discover a new vison for yourself.
CreativityPlaybook.com

My Journey

My Journey

"I live by my quote every day: 'Quietness is one of the most precious elements in nurturing the mind to activate its powers.'

Tune out to tune in. Our world has become busier and noisier each day. Only when there's quietness, can we tap into our higher-self to activate our mind powers and maximize our true potentials. Quietness brings peace from within. Seek not more external influences but powers from within to cultivate your full potentials."

Linda Tomai Duong is the Amazon #1 International Bestseller and Award-Winning Author of *Connection: Currency to Happiness*, an Inspirational Speaker, Life & Parenting Coach, and Thought Leader on Happiness and Connection. https://m.facebook.com/linkcoaching.com.au/

My Journey

My Journey

"A friend who betrayed me years ago was on my mind. Wanting to let go and forgive, I closed my eyes, visualized him, and focused on our interaction. I believed I would never see him again. Miraculously when I opened my eyes, he was standing before me! He wanted forgiveness as much as I wanted to give it to him.

Forgiving those who betray us benefits us as well as the ones who inflicted it."

Thomas Carelli is a native Bronx, New Yorker, Computer Tech at Fordham University, and Facilitator of teachings on *A Course in Miracles*, Edgar Cayce, and Abraham's LoA. TheCourse@gmail.com

My Journey

— _DAY 82_ —

My Journey

"I was told to become a Technician Advisor and sell everything to everybody. This resulted in frustration and overwhelm. You can't be everything to everybody because you'll serve no one well.

To truly be successful, you must become an authority in your marketplace. In order to do this, you need to get clear on who you serve, the one problem that you solve, and the solution you can deliver to them that will change their lives."

Daniel Hanzelka helps Financial Advisors scale their business to get more clients, make more money, have more freedom and make a bigger impact in the world.
ResetYourMoney.com

My Journey

My Journey

*"Awakening your Wisdom is the alchemical process of releasing limiting beliefs and unserving emotional patterns that are keeping you from making the quantum shift and strengthening the inner bond with your True Self. Give yourself permission to <u>courageously</u> and <u>compassionately</u> transform these patterns. Experience life and be experienced as your True Self in every   action and reaction. **Live your truth. BE your divine, True Self** and embrace it in all its wonder and beauty."*

Crystal Cockerham guides women through the spiritual alchemical process of transformation connecting them with their inner wisdom to access their divine truth and live a joy-filled life.   <u>WisdomAwakens.com</u>

My Journey

_____

_____

_____

_____

_____

_____

_____

_____

_____

_____

_____

_____

_____

My Journey

"Believe in Yourself. Understand and embrace your potential. Each of us has enormous potential to succeed and grow. Many of us fail to use that potential. When we Believe and own who we are and what we can do, we can achieve awesome results. Acknowledge who you are, acknowledge your expertise, acknowledge how far you can go, and acknowledge how awesome you are. Throw off those limiting beliefs that stop you – be all you were destined to be."

Trish Springsteen, Australia's Leading Expert in Empowering Introverts, Speaker, Mentor, Multi-International Award Winner, International best-selling Author and Radio Host. Co-Founder/Owner of Trischel – creating confident communicators.   TrishSpringsteen.com

My Journey

— _DAY 85_ —

My Journey

— *DAY 86* —

"The word 'how' used to literally stop me in my tracks. I'd stop myself from doing what needed to be done, wasting my time trying to figure out the un-figure-out-able. When I finally let go of that need - that resistance - things started to move. The 'how' is not up to us to figure out. Focus on your 'why' and move towards your dream. God will take care of the 'how.'"

C. E. Shaw, Author, Reiki Master, and Equine Therapist.
HorseMomShaw@yahoo.ca

My Journey

— _DAY 86_ —

My Journey

"Every second, of every minute, of every day we have a choice. We can either be the person moaning about how the world is full of pain, injustice and tragedy, or we can be the person who takes action to turn the world into one which inspires, motivates and loves without conviction.

If you're living your life from the perspective of the first person - consider this to be your wake-up call.

Choose now. Choose wisely."

Katie Woodland, Developmental Psychologist, helps entrepreneurs overcome stress, depression and anxiety so that they can create the life of their dreams by building the business they love.   KatieWoodland.co.uk

My Journey

— _DAY 87_ —

My Journey

"I became aware of intuition early on and have been using it all my life. When you start to consciously choose to become aware of and pay attention to your intuition, you can achieve your desired results. Consciously listening to your 'gut' can bring the means to uncover a new path to success. Every morning, take a few moments to ask, 'What is my intuition/gut telling me today?' and follow it."

Lumi Vasile as a Spiritual Mentor and Transformational Catalyst, helps people to create and manifest their dream life in direct connection and cooperation with Spirit. JourneyIntoTheLight.com

My Journey

— _DAY 88_ —

My Journey

"The people who say you can't make money from writing are the people who didn't try hard enough. How do I know this? Because I was already making way more money from writing than I ever had in a full-time job before I learned it was 'impossible'.

If you want to write, don't let anyone tell you can't do it, because if you're willing to put the work in, you CAN do it."

Deborah A. Stansil is a full-time Writer and Blogger who is best known for her love of the horror genre.
MyRandomMusings.co.uk

My Journey

— <u>*DAY 89*</u> —

My Journey

"'It will all work out in the end' is what fueled my entrepreneurial journey. After years of financial struggle, health issues and lack of a deep love relationship, I realized I could step into my own faith in myself to do anything I thought possible. Today I'm a highly successful speaker, author and entrepreneur making great money doing what I love. You can do this too if you believe in yourself."

The JumpStart Your Biz Coach, **Katrina Sawa** kicks her clients and their businesses into high gear, turning their inspiration and ideas into smooth-running moneymaking businesses. JumpstartYourMarketing.com

My Journey

— <u>*DAY 90*</u> —

My Journey

— *DAY 91* —

"You are so amazing and beautiful! By allowing yourself to believe that you can be, do or have anything you want in the world is the greatest gift you can give yourself and thus the world.

What would you like to do TODAY to ALLOW the best version of YOU to be present? Loving you and loving what you do is key. Shine on!"

Lynda Dyer Msc, featured in *The Secret*, Int'l Speaker, Certified Professional NLP Trainer, and Author of 9 #1 Int'l Best-Selling, Award-Winning books. MindPowerGlobal.com.au

My Journey

— _DAY 91_ —

My Journey

"People often ask me if they can share the concepts I teach. Of course! It is all about TRANSMISSION. Everything you teach, you learned it first, and channeled it often. Then, it matured within your mind and cells to the point of inspiring you to share your unique experience with others. That's what the world needs: models of experience, as imperfect as the human being and as deep and true as they can be."

Marcelle della Faille, Best-Selling Author, Law of Attraction Mentor, well-known for her training programs about making peace with money and developing a thriving business. LoveandMoneyAlchemy.com/free-chapter-make-peace-with-money

My Journey

— _DAY 92_ —

My Journey

"I was browsing through a gift shop and what caught my eye was a wall plaque that said, 'Live a Great Story.' As I considered the impact of living a great story, I realized this could also mean sharing a powerful message. If you look deep within, you will find a story that others need to hear. Do you know that ONE story can influence, impact and even transform millions of lives? Why not yours?"

Linda Olson is a Speaker, Story Expert, #1 Int'l Best-Selling Author, and Founder of Wealth Through Stories. WealthThroughStories.com

My Journey

_____

_____

_____

_____

_____

_____

_____

_____

_____

_____

_____

_____

_____

_____

_____

_____

— _DAY 93_ —

My Journey

"If one seeks to gain knowledge, one must apply what one already knows. For it is in the application of knowledge that deeper wisdom resides. A seeker of knowledge will forever seek but never find. A practitioner of knowledge will gain the wisdom they seek. To be ignorant of knowledge is one thing, to ignore it is another. So use what you know or be doomed to ignorance. For wisdom is knowledge applied well."

Carol Little, Public Speaker and Master Trainer draws on 15+ years of experience to deliver practical and accessible tools to improve her clients public speaking skills. LittleTrainingCompany.com

My Journey

— _DAY 94_ —

My Journey

"The promises we whisper to ourselves are often the most precious - but usually the ones we ignore.

We must build evidence we can do what we say and finish what we start, so we can say 'Yes' wholeheartedly to the bigger things.

Journaling our quietest intentions is the first step. And once we've committed them to paper, we must take action. Listen to the whispers. Write them down. And bring your dreams to life."

Cath Grey helps professionals reconnect with their vision, purpose and direction, and supports them in implementing specific strategies to achieve their desired outcomes.
CathGrey.com

My Journey

My Journey

"Be true to yourself. Make the choice to live your life with integrity. When you are true to yourself, you lead with your values and your message aligns with your heart. People strive for authenticity in every person they meet and in every business they reach. They will still follow you no matter if you change or upgrade your business because you've built your connections based on who you are, not on what you do."

Juracy Johnson, Best-Selling Author, Professional Life Coach, Founder of Professional Women's Network Mexico, guiding Latin American Women to learn to love themselves and develop a strong, feminine Personal Presence.
Juracy.Johnson@gmail.com

My Journey

My Journey

"*In the 1980s in Bedford Stuyvasent, Brooklyn, New York, my father resembled a mafia movie character. Guns, days in prison and gambling spots, while I was often awoken to the sound of thousands of dollars rustling under his fingertips. The normal, quieter life in the suburbs with a father similar to a TV sitcom wouldn't become a reality until he became elderly. Time healed wounds, and his last eight years brought happy, healthy memories.*"

Shirley Jusino is a Global Sciences Foundation Certified Life Coach. She is also a 3 time Int'l Best-Selling Author.
ShirleyJusino@ymail.com

My Journey

— *DAY 97* —

My Journey

"Far too many times in today's society, people make the mistake of labeling an introvert as 'anti-social' or 'strange'.

An introvert needs time for solitude and introspection to process their ideas, their lives. Only then can they create, shine, succeed and change the fast-paced world around them.

This is how your favorite song, television show, movie, technology or artwork was created. Respecting and accepting introverts' time can help the world evolve."

Gabriel R. Gonzalez is a native Brooklyn, New York freelance Graphic Artist and Art Specialist teaching special needs adults, as well as children.
facebook.com/Gabriel.Gonzalez.14019

My Journey

— *<u>DAY 98</u>* —

My Journey

"A diagnosis of two Stage 3 cancers requires a partnership of your mind, body and spirit. All that head chatter! It's like a freight train – loud and difficult to ignore.

It tells you how hard it is or how rotten you feel; your emotions follow suit and then your body is very close behind. Before you know it, you really DO feel like crap!

Writing is cathartic. There is peace there."

Debra Wilson Guttas, HTP, MID-Life Transition Doula, Reiki Master, Speaker, and Best-Selling Author of *7 Keys to Coping with Cancer - How You Can Feel Good AND THRIVE (from someone who's been there)*. <u>ConduitForSelfHealing.com</u>

My Journey

— <u>DAY 99</u> —

My Journey

"Understand that the mind is an incredibly complex and infinite place. Its potential to create and invent is unlimited. Know that mind power; or rather, our ability to control our mind is an amazing resource. It can control our fears, and radically affect our determination. It can shape our beliefs and our faith. Be brilliant!"

DeNise N. Gore, Certified Holistic Health Coach, Lifestyle Strategist, Author, Speaker & Founder of Radiant Brilliance – a personal development company.   RadiantBrilliance.com

My Journey

— *DAY 100* —

My Journey

"In today's society, negative forms of discrimination, whether it is in the home, workplace or place of worship should never be accepted. People should refuse giving monetary support to those who do discriminate. Inequality is not an acceptable way of treating any humans. A possible "1000 Years of Peace" is coming with the universally found Golden Rule of Equal Respect and Concern where there is no scarcity and conflict is nonexistent. Praise The Creator of All!"

Betty C. Dudney, Retired Medical Technologist, Author, Activist for Peace Vigils, Civil Rights, Farm Workers Unions and Co-Founder of the non-profit Golden Rule Family and WorldwideHumanRights.org.   WorldwideHumanRights.org

My Journey

— _DAY 101_ —

My Journey

"We are always in the state of undergoing pain, worry and distress for the most part of our lives. It's not because we want it that way, but it's a reactive response to what it is happening in our life. In order to heal our anticipated difficulties or catastrophe, it requires retraining of a new mindset, a new routine, a new awareness and a new accountability. We must empower our happiness by taking AC-TIONS!"

Margaret Tran is the Author of *The ACTIONS*, a speaker, organizer and advocate *Random Act of Kindness* (RAK), and mindset/spiritual and energy healing coach.
NewMindsetNewResults.com

My Journey

My Journey

"Following a cross-country road a century old may not be as well-trod a path as you think! Over time, people build new roads and choose alternative routes that benefit their journeys. But with support from others, patience, and luck, I found an authentic yellow brick road that led to my dream today (it's true!). Sometimes finding things long forgotten is what brings you to be your best self today and in the future."

Cecelia "Cece" Otto, professional singer, author, historian and founder of An American Songline®, which shares America's history through song and story.   AmericanSongline.com

My Journey

— _DAY 103_ —

My Journey

"They say healthy is an 'outfit that looks different on everyone'. When embarking on your journey to health and wellness, don't be afraid to break free from the pack when trying to find what works for you. Be brave and blaze your own trail. You are unlike anyone else and your healthy lifestyle is yours to design. You have to live it each day, so be sure you can love it each day!"

Jenni Samano, Founder & CEO of H3 Coaching Services, The Happy Humble Health Coach, Life Empowerment Coach and Author.   H3CoachingServices.com

My Journey

— _DAY 104_ —

My Journey

"What is something that you've always wanted to do, but you never seem to bring yourself to accomplish it? You tell yourself it can't be done for one reason or another? That's called a limiting belief, and I'm here to tell you that you don't have to listen to that voice that tells you that you can't. Overcome that voice, do what you have always wanted, EMERGE and become who you were meant to be!"

Cody Wooten, Founder of LoCo Coyote Enterprises, Leadership Coach, Speaker and Teacher, helps others overcome their limiting beliefs.   LoCoCoyote.Enterprises

My Journey

— _DAY 105_ —

My Journey

"Once you love yourself unconditionally and accept yourself wholly, your life will begin to fill with abundance. Kindness, understanding, and self-care will lead you to true fulfillment as they allow you to step into who you really are. When you find yourself, you will find your purpose. As a result, other aspects of your life will fall into place as you align yourself with your purpose and God's plan for you."

Alina Vasilenko, Author of the "Mighty and Brennon" book series, a comedy about cats written under the pen name Alexis, assists people in writing their stories.
Alexis@WrittenStoryPlanet.com

My Journey

_____

_____

_____

_____

_____

_____

_____

_____

_____

_____

_____

_____

_____

_____

My Journey

"*Humpty Dumpty has been an allegory defining most of my life. I felt shattered, scattered, and splattered.*

In mid-life, I gathered my mess and put Humpty back together, Feeling more whole as each shell piece fit into place. Finally Complete, I climbed back up. Then realized... I DIDN'T BELONG THERE.

Jumped off the wall, re-shattered the shell, and discovered I was whole like a hard-boiled egg and the mess of my life was really egg salad."

D. Crystal Johnson is an Award-Winning Int'l Best-Selling Contributing Author, Certified Life Coach and Facilitator who helps people become the best they can Be.
D.CrystalJohnson2@gmail.com

My Journey

— _DAY 107_ —

My Journey

"Keep going no matter what, and trust in Divine timing. I stopped and started my recent novel, "Crossing the Line," many times and almost gave up on it. In the end, I was so glad I didn't and realized that there was something valuable being revealed in every pause. The end result exceeded my expectations.

Every rose blooms in its own time; so will you and your book. Keep at it and never stop believing!"

Ellen Wolfson Valladares, Award-Winning Author and Freelance Writer. Her newest release, *Crossing the Line*, is an intriguing, mystical novel about friendship, fate, and the courage to believe.   EllenValladares.com

My Journey

— _DAY 108_ —

My Journey

"We must learn to 'let go'. We must take regular time out to listen to our own silence and become aware of the present moment. Our story is not the only story. When we respect ourselves, we can respect others. When we respect others, we can listen to their story. Then we learn how to open our hearts and minds to understand tolerance for differences in the opinions of others."

Margaret E. Lawrence, Personal Development Facilitator, is on a mission to 'help other people perform effectively' through the development of confidence and positive mindset. Lawrence.Margaret53@gmail.com

My Journey

My Journey

"I was told, 'This is as good as you can expect life to get,' when I was recovering from childhood abuse and still in a lot of pain. My inner voice said, 'No, I don't accept this!' Now, I have surpassed everyone's expectations, including my own.

Don't let anyone else define who you are. You were born for something amazing and you can soar as high as you can imagine. Never give up on yourself!"

Heidi McElvaine, Coach, Healer, Angel Connector, Author, and Founder of Ascending Heights Enterprises. She empowers you to find and be your true authentic self! AscendingHeights.com

My Journey

— <u>*DAY 110*</u> —

My Journey

"My coach advised me that a book would be the best business card. 'Can you finish it in 2 months before our speaking event?' My mouth said 'yes', my head asked 'are you crazy?!' Once I sat down and just did it, I was surprised at how easily it flowed out of me. Is it perfect? Nope. Yet here I am a published author which gives me more business credibility plus helps me serve many. I hope this inspires you to just start writing!"

Pamela James, Published Author, Business Process Expert, Founder of 365 Living Well and The Project is You that focus on different aspects of living your 'BEST of YOU' life! 365LivingWell.com

My Journey

My Journey

— *DAY 112* —

"From Chains to Change expresses the glorious Breakthrough in our current circumstances we all too often long for. Resiliency teaches us that we have faced seemingly insurmountable Dilemmas in the past, yet we ultimately claimed our Freedom. Difficult times stretch us. Recalling what Giants we faced and how we overcame them will fuel our next Victory. After the Dark Night of the Soul, our Heroic Journey finds us at Home in our Heart once again."

Sally Holland, Life Coach to Adults in Transition. Celebrating your Difference. Re-Visioning your Life Purpose. Creative Solutions with Surprising Clarity.   KeepItSimpleSally.com

My Journey

My Journey

"What if you knew that you are the Heroine of your life?

And that every single dragon you have slain, every mountain you have climbed and every tear you have shed, has blessed you with hidden depths of wisdom, understanding and compassion for yourself and the world?

And what if the soul purpose of your life is simply to love and acknowledge yourself as the perfection that you are? Would you live your life differently?"

Caroline Ryan, a multi-dimensional traveler and explorer; a questioner of truths; an opener of pathways; a connector and amplifier of people and possibilities for planetary wholeness. TheLegacyArchitect.com

My Journey

— _DAY 113_ —

My Journey

"On my life's journey, I've come to the realization that we are all different threads in this great tapestry called Humanity. Most of us are committed to weaving beautiful imagery with our strands - love, compassion, mercy. But others offer no more than a knotted, gnarly ugliness - racism, hatred, intolerance. This compels me to try even harder, love even deeper, and do more to soften my footsteps. Redouble your efforts - become the change."

Lily-Ann MacDonald, is an Award-Winning Writer, Author, and Editor with her company Write-Rightly Full Service Editing and Writing Agency.   Write-Rightly.com

My Journey

....

....

....

....

....

....

....

....

....

....

....

....

....

....

....

....

....

— <u>*DAY 114*</u> —

My Journey

"Are you suspicious of everything, or are you just keeping your eyes and ears open? There are many good opportunities awaiting you, yet perils abound too. Healthy skepticism can help you avoid being scammed or cheated, but cynicism prevents you from seeing genuine possibilities for improving life for you and your loved ones. So keep your head up high, be aware of your surroundings, and learn to discern a gift from a grift."

Joe Libby, International Speaker and Entertainer from San Antonio, TX. Joe utilizes his expert knowledge of magic and deception to educate on the dangers of cons and scams.

JoeLibbySeminars.com   (Photo by Jacklen Taylor, Outlaw Photography)

My Journey

— _DAY 115_ —

My Journey

" *'All things yield to the proper combination of technique and persistence. Especially persistence.'*
~ from Guidance

Whenever I've felt stymied by a massively stubborn 'thing,' this Spirit message has rekindled my creativity and recharged my determination.

Persistence synergizes the Yang of willpower with the Yin of trust. Inspired Technique + Persistence = Unstoppable Forces no 'thing' can withstand! What 'thing' will now yield to YOU?"

Susan V. Sinclair, The Unboxed Oracle and Founder of GraceFlow Healing Arts, reawakens people's intuitive empowerment and spiritual sovereignty through workshops, Deep Soul Readings, and Soul-Deep Energy Healing.
SusanSinclair.org

My Journey

_____

_____

_____

_____

_____

_____

_____

_____

_____

_____

_____

My Journey

"At a time when my life was falling apart, I realized I could not control what was going on around me, but I could control myself. My feelings, thoughts and responses were mine to choose, that is what I was in control of. I decided I didn't have to stay where I was and I didn't have to feel powerless. That day I stopped being a victim and chose to step into my power and you can too!"

Taflyn Allen, owner of Taflyn Allen Coaching. Early Childhood Development practitioner and confidence coach to parents of young children with sensory processing disorder and behavioral challenges.   TaflynAllenCoaching.com

My Journey

_____

_____

_____

_____

_____

_____

_____

_____

_____

_____

_____

_____

_____

_____

_____

_____

— <u>DAY 117</u> —

My Journey

"Why do so many people feel that for-giveness doesn't work? We either blame ourselves or decide that 'it won't work' for us. Sometimes we fear that forgiving is the same as condoning and will leave us total-ly vulnerable to pain. Yet, the crucial ques-tion 'Who needs to forgive me?' is rarely asked. When all three elements: forgiving others and self and seeking the need for forgiveness from others, will mind/body/spiritual healing manifest."

Patricia Margaitis PhD LCSW CNC DAAIM FAPA is an Integrative Holistic Psychotherapist and Wellness Life Coach specializing in mind/body/spiritual health for personal growth. WomansWellness@HealthOnYourMind.com

My Journey

— <u>DAY 118</u> —

My Journey

"My 77 years has had many ups and downs however, one of the most powerful phases has been learning that I don't have to let fear or what others think stop me from achieving what I want and for nearly 30 years, having the honor of teaching the same thing to other women. When you believe in yourself, you can achieve whatever you want. Never allow doubts and fears to hold you back."

Hazel Palache, aka The Mindset Mentor, is a certified Success Coach, Clinical Hypnotherapist, NLP Practitioner, Stress Management Counselor, an Amazon Best-Selling Author and Motivational Speaker.   LiveYourAbundantLife.com

My Journey

My Journey

"I accept my book is not for every publisher, editor or audience. However, I also knew my book did have a right publisher, editor and audience. I just had to find them. So, when my book was not picked up immediately, I kept trying. Sure it scared me and poked at my sensitive writerly feelings but I knew the right opportunity existed, because I poured everything into my writing to make it great. I found them. Keep Writing!"

Devin Galaudet, publisher of InTheKnowTraveler.com and the author of the best-selling memoir *10,000 Miles with my Dead Father's Ashes*.   DevinGalaudet.com

My Journey

My Journey

"When I began writing my first book at age 26, I felt like an impostor. Who was I to claim to be an author, an expert? One morning a life-changing thought came to me that I wrote down and taped to my computer, where it lived for many years: 'I do not write because I am a writer; I write because I have something to say. What do <u>you</u> have to say?'"

Dr. Judith Boice is a naturopathic physician, acupuncturist and #1 international best-selling author. She is the Chief Vitality Officer and Keeper of the Green Medicine Chest. DrJudithBoice.com

My Journey

My Journey

"You only have one life to live right now. If you spend your time berating yourself for past mistakes and filling your days with guilt, you will never be able to live the life of your dreams.

Once you realize this is your life and you are in charge, your world becomes amazing and light; free from angst, anger and worry. Don't wait to discover yourself; start living your authentically awesome life today."

Michael Shook, the internet's most positive writer. Publisher at <u>MichaelShook.com</u>, home of the internet's most positive personal growth programs, products and courses.

My Journey

— _DAY 122_ —

My Journey

"Be yourself. Write in your own way, in your own voice - like only you can. There is no right or wrong way to write. Seek positive, encouraging people to interact with. Ignore those negative people who are too afraid to pursue their own dreams, so they feel obligated to dash yours. Sometimes this person is yourself. Refuse to listen to this negative voice inside. Keep looking ahead, writing, dreaming. You will succeed!"

Allyssa (A.A.) Riley, is the creator of The Allyssa Method of Living Right, Author of the *Key of Aramath* and magazine articles, Editor and Holistic Lifestyle Coach. AllyssaMethod.com

My Journey

— <u>DAY 123</u> —

My Journey

— *DAY 124* —

"My parents gave me six horseback riding lessons for Christmas when I was 12 years old. I was a horse crazed girl who was ecstatic when I opened the gift. I started my lessons by being told that I was too short and I'd never be a good rider. My tenacity drove me to a 25-year long riding career that ended training and competing dressage. Never let anyone take your dreams away!"

Lynn Herkes, Publisher, Writer, retired Dressage Trainer, retired Aerospace Engineer, Travel Blogger, Video Creator, Website Designer, Marketer, Freelancer, and Business Consultant. <u>WowSuccessTeam.com</u>

My Journey

— _DAY 124_ —

My Journey

— DAY 125 —

"When I think about getting more stuff done, it quickly leads to questioning which things are most important, and why it matters to do them at all. Think of one area of your life that has been most neglected over the past year. How important is it to you? Allow your daily priorities to be guided by your core values, and you will start experiencing a new level of productivity, regardless of your current role."

Jacques Soiné, is the Author and Founder of Exponential Productivity, "Start multiplying the results you love in your life." Jacques@JacquesSoine.com

My Journey

_____

_____

_____

_____

_____

_____

_____

_____

_____

_____

_____

_____

_____

_____

_____

_____

— _DAY 125_ —

My Journey

"I've often heard the phrase, "Your mess is your message." Finally taking the lead to turn my mess around has completely transformed my life and career. My inability to take responsibility for my needs, thoughts and emotions resulted in isolation and splintered relationships. Finding forgiveness for myself, as well as others, has led me on a new path paved with grace, love, and best of all honest communication."

Colleen Elaine is a Speaker, Empowerment Coach, Author of her new book, *Holding Forgiveness Hostage*, and Co-founder of Notúre: Self-care made simple. Noture-SelfCare.com

My Journey

— <u>DAY 126</u> —

My Journey

"My journal, a loving companion and resource for my deepest thoughts and dreams. It's allowed those visions to surface, often spilling freely from my mind in a flow of tears, enthusiasm and release.

Ideas for future seminars, even books, sprouted from a conversation with myself revealing my hopes and fears. By journaling, they became real. I could sort through the web of my life and work, and get clarity to courageously and successfully move forward."

Dr. Jo Anne White, is a #1 International Bestselling Author, Speaker, Certified Coach, Executive Producer and Host of Power Your Life Radio and TV, and Founder of Power Your Life Network . <u>DrJoAnneWhite.com</u>

My Journey

— _DAY 127_ —

My Journey

"The best way to handle challenges in life is to ACCEPT Adversities! BEGIN Battling! CONQUER Challenges! Problems do not fix themselves; difficulties are not destroyed unless the situation is faced head on. We can triumph over tragedies. Don't survive in a valley when we can thrive on a mountaintop of the world. After dominating adversities in the game life, we can celebrate the thrill of victory knowing we stood tall and prevailed as winners."

Dr. James M. Perdue, Quadriplegic from a football game, Educator, Championship Coach, Author, and Speaker on ABC's of Perseverance: Accept Adversities, Begin Battle, and Conquer Challenges.
ProfessorofPerseverance.com

My Journey

— _DAY 128_ —

My Journey

"My life is calm, secure, and beautiful. I **LOVE** *knowing I have the power to create the existence I desire because I release the past. The* **present is special**, *and* **I embrace every moment**.

Today, my goal is to take hold of the present and live it to its fullest.

So, I release my past to make plenty of room for my present. Life is beautiful because the present is here in its full glory. Yours can be too!"

Kathryn Jingling: Empowering Women with Mental Illness - Build Emotional Wellness through Education and Support -to Live Their BEST Life.
Kathryn@KatzAwesomeLifeJourney.com

My Journey

— _DAY 129_ —

My Journey

"Follow your heart; it knows the way.

Growing up, I was told not to listen to my heart because it could mislead me, so I let my mind tell me what to do. While I am grateful for the knowledge I gained, my happiness came when I followed my heart and heeded the call of my passion to lead others on their path to purpose.

When you listen to the call of your heart, it leads to happiness."

Laura Leighty Wade, Founder of Thrive by Heart, Soul to Goal Guide, Certified Facilitator and Writer, guides you to consciously create a life you love.   ThriveByHeart.com

My Journey

— _DAY 130_ —

My Journey

"Whether it is loud and proud, or whispered and subtle, or gentle and strong, or brash and bold... find your unique style and share your message. You get to be unapologetically you, without another course, certification, product, or program. There is someone, somewhere, waiting for you, needing you, ready to learn from you and you have everything you need within you to be that part of yourself. You got this! Who will you be today?"

Patty Rose, Author, Speaker, Empowerment Coach, Founder of Create.Build.Share.™, Dance Strong™, The Inspirations System™, inspires creative entrepreneurial women to create online businesses that succeed.   PattyRose.com

My Journey

— _DAY 131_ —

My Journey

"You don't have to do everything. You don't have to be everything. Know those things that are your strengths, AND your weaknesses. Then gather to you those people that have your weaknesses as strengths, and build something great together. Collect smiles and laughter and revisit them often.

Life doesn't always go the way we want, sometimes it's better, but growing pains usually hurt. This too shall pass. Remember your light and love, and move forward."

Lynn Jasmin is a #1 International Best-Selling Author, Speaker, Corporate Training and Stress Reduction Specialist. RelaxedFreedom.com

My Journey

My Journey

"Make money fall in love with you.

When you imagine your money as a real, flesh and blood person, worthy of your deepest admiration, you embark on an amazing, love-at-first-sight affair of the heart.

Pennies on the ground are like chocolates on your pillow ."

Morgana Rae is a sought after teacher, speaker and pioneer in personal development and is widely regarded to be the world's leading Relationship with Money coach. MorganaRae.com

My Journey

_____

_____

_____

_____

_____

_____

_____

_____

_____

_____

_____

_____

_____

_____

My Journey

"Last year to my surprise and delight, I began channeling Rainbow Chakra Angels, who've come to help us connect with our chakras and become in-lightened about the beautiful rainbow within. They said everyone has their own personal team. 'We want you to embrace all that you are, and your chakras are a much underrated way to do this. That's why we've come, to inspire and guide you. You need simply ask.' How vibrant is your inner rainbow?"

Alexandria Barker is an Author, Speaker, Reiki Master, Crystal Therapist, Akashic Records Consultant who helps you turn the life you HAVE into a life you'll LOVE.
AlexandriaBarker.com

My Journey

My Journey

"Pain is horrible. But sometimes pain is necessary. In my case, pain is what it took to make me change careers when The Universe had something much better and different in mind... and I wasn't listening.

If you are experiencing pain, you may want to take some time and evaluate what you are doing at those times. What are you thinking about? And most importantly, are you receiving messages from The Universe and aren't listening?"

Tracy Una Wagner, CHT, an Intuitive Transpersonal Guide, and Energy Alchemist can be found creating magic around her home in the mystical Pacific Northwest nestled amongst the trees!   TracyUnaWagner.com

My Journey

— <u>*DAY 135*</u> —

My Journey

"The two worst things that happened to me had to happen to bring me to my best accomplishments. Without the divorce, I would have never discovered how capable I am. Without a fire destroying my business building, I wouldn't have built a bigger building, giving me room to create something entirely new which took me into the Minnesota Women Business Owners Hall of Fame. Be open to possibilities when the Universe opens an unexpected door!"

Lorelei Kraft, #1 Best-Selling Author, Speaker and Serial Entrepreneur. Only 2% of women-owned businesses reach a million in revenues, and Lorelei created two that did.
KraftKeys.com

My Journey

My Journey

"You can Create & Manifest a Life You Love!™

Your thoughts, feelings, emotions, and beliefs create a vibrational frequency that will either attract or repel what you desire. You can attract your desires by shifting your thoughts, raising your vibration, and expanding your conscious awareness to become a Manifesting Magnet to Attract & Create Your Desires.™

When your desires are in alignment with the higher vibrations of love, joy, and gratitude your life will transform."

Donna Burgher, Founder/Creator of Create & Manifest a Life You Love!™, #1 Best-Selling Co-Author, Advanced Manifesting Mentor, and Master Your Mindset Coach. DonnaBurgher.com

My Journey

— _DAY 137_ —

My Journey

"Know that one of your greatest gifts and powers is your ability to create. In fact, you are the artist of your life; and your life is a masterpiece in the making. So, go for it with all you got.

Paint your masterpiece in the most exuberant colors and in the most distinctive style possible and this way celebrate life. Recognize that by making your dreams real, you contribute to something much larger than yourself."

Birgit Langhammer, Art Teacher, Artist and Author of the forthcoming book, *Your Life is Art: Make Every Day a Masterpiece.* BirgitLanghammer.com

My Journey

— _DAY 138_ —

My Journey

"*A tribe got a new well. The elders (all men) decided the water would be reserved for livestock and crops. However, the women rebelled, surrounded the well, and took control, wanting the water for bathing, cooking, and the children. The chief said, 'I guess we forgot to ask the women their opinion.' Work for a world where it would be unthinkable to disregard women and make decisions without their valuable and unique perspective.*"

Lois Kerschen, retired educator and editor, wrote *American Proverbs About Women* and continues political/social justice activism and the promotion of her design at dualitycross.com.
LoisKerschen@gmail.com

My Journey

_____
_____
_____
_____
_____
_____
_____
_____
_____
_____
_____
_____
_____
_____
_____

My Journey

"I live 'accidentally on purpose' by maintaining a vision of success that encompasses my spiritual, intellectual, social and economic impact. I pursue this confidently, making value-based decisions even if the outcome initially seems negative. I just sleep better that way. Living this way, I have found I always leave people better than when I met them; and happy 'accidents' have followed - no puppeteering necessary."

Lela Woodard, Speaker and Founder of My Inside Out Life.
Pikhe@icloud.com

My Journey

— _DAY 140_ —

My Journey

"The journey we embark on as humans is very special. All of our journeys are filled with experiences that bring out a variety of emotions in us, which then creates a pathway. All our different pathways lead us all to the same destination. So why not make the journey through our pathways we create a beautiful one?"

Mental Health Advocate, **Alysha Gill** strives to be the best version of herself and hopes to help as many people as she can who face similar struggles.   Alysha.Gill17@gmail.com

My Journey

My Journey

"Motivation gathered through listening to motivational speeches will fade away within few days. This is why you need to motivate yourself daily. And there is no stronger motivating factor than daily accomplishment of a step, that empowers you to confidently advance in the direction of your dreams. Making the small steps that most people are reluctant to do will let you live the life most people will keep only dreaming of."

Ivan Petarnichki, NLP, Hypnotherapy, Timeline Therapy Practitioner, Spiritual Technologies Trainer, Mental Edge Mastery Expert and Bulgaria's Best-Selling Author of Emotional Freedom and PTSD Recovery Books.
MentalEdgeMastery.com

My Journey

My Journey

" 'Share your vision and the universe will conspire to make it happen' is advice that I received from an old boss of mine. Taking this advice made me realize that you have to bravely speak your vision into existence, even if your voice shakes while doing so. Holding your vision inside doesn't give it the soil, air and water it needs to grow and blossom into reality. Who will you share your vision with today?"

Jenny Garrett is a UK based Award Winning Coach, Author & Leadership Trainer. She's passionate about supporting women and young people to realize their potential. JennyGarrett.Global

My Journey

My Journey

— *DAY 144* —

"My simple ways to stay happy wherever you are: Befriend your imperfections. Never stop dreaming. Always relax before work. Plan your fun and free time to avoid tiredness and frustration and have more energy and motivation. Be creative. Work out regularly to release stress and prevent depression. Try something new and surprising every day. Nonstandard acting will chase boredom away forever and allow you to regain control over your life. Always celebrate even smallest successes."

Agata Szkiela, Culture Transition Success Coach empowering strong expat and diplomat women worldwide to thrive personally and professionally in new cultures.
about.me/AgataSzkiela

My Journey

My Journey

"I was raised by two loving parents in a time when you got an education, worked hard, and waited until retirement to collect social security and travel. At 21, I lost my mother. My father was a good provider but a workaholic. He'd never go on vacation without constantly calling work while away. From his example, I learned not to wait to do what you love and that travel enriches the soul."

Kyle Bruening (aka Captain Kyle), Luxury Travel Advisor, Owner of Cruise Finder Inc., Publisher and Author Cruise-In-Touch, seen on ABC, NBC, CBS, MSNBC and CNN. info@CruiseFinderInc.com

My Journey

— _DAY 145_ —

My Journey

"A piece of advice for your younger self: **Choice**. You always have a choice. It's a superpower that can never be taken away from you. It doesn't matter what is going on in life, you have a choice on how you feel which can change the outcome. Your power of choice defines and shapes your perspective. It's so simple yet over-looked so easily. It's the game changer. <u>You have a choice</u>."

Serena Dallas is Author of *How I Got Out of My Own Way*, Speaker and Motivational Expert for those who are ready to own their lives.   <u>SerenaDallas.com</u>

My Journey

_____

_____

_____

_____

_____

_____

_____

_____

_____

_____

_____

_____

_____

_____

_____

_____

_____

My Journey

"How have you captured the power of your unique journey? I assure you, there is significant reason for this question. As shocking as this message may be: life is short and no one is promised tomorrow.

It's easy to dismiss this chilling notion. After my near-death experience, that was no longer an option. The guiding force became savor every moment. Highlighting gratitude and experiences in a journal is a guaranteed way to carpe diem - seize the day!"

Dr. Tianna Conte, Transformational Best-Selling Author and trailblazing blend of Mystic and Scientist. With 40 years of expertise, she empowers self-evolution by re-awakening innate guidance and power.   YourGPSCode.com

My Journey

— _DAY 147_ —

My Journey

"Writing in a journal can be like speaking to a best friend, or to a beloved and held by your own words. Thoughts surface that we are not often aware of before putting them down on paper.

Through journaling, we are able to see how pieces of our lives fit together; individual circumstances find meaning in the whole. Even pain when expressed can reveal the underlying blessings. To journal is a gift."

Mary Azima Jackson, MDiv, DMin - Azima's expertise focuses on life's rites of passage through song, meditation, and ceremony. She is an ordained Interfaith Minister with a Masters from Yale. <u>AHouseofLight.com</u>

My Journey

— _DAY 148_ —

My Journey

"Something grabs your attention on this journey of life. An idea that seems too good to ignore. A stiff neck that competes for your focus. A phone call you feel compelled to make. Pay attention. Consider taking action even if it feels impractical or outrageous. What would happen if you listened to and acted upon these callings? How would you change? How would your life change?"

Sharon Roemmel, BSW, ACC, E-RYT, helps women who are excited about their purpose become equally passionate about taking care of their number one asset — themselves. PracticallyEnlightenedYou.com

My Journey

_____

_____

_____

_____

_____

_____

_____

_____

_____

_____

_____

_____

_____

_____

— _DAY 149_ —

My Journey

"What if?
You are more than you believe.
Listen to the secrets whispered in your dreams.
Awaken to the possibility that you are more.
Make room for a new dream to form.
A new vision to present itself to you.
Make room for more by letting go of fear.
Invite love into your life.
It only takes one small step.
One simple choice.
It has already begun with these words –
What if?"

Linda Valente is a Transformational Coach who specializes in working with women who have experienced abusive relationships. LindaValenteCoaching.com

My Journey

— _DAY 150_ —

My Journey

"Never give up. The Power exists in your mind to reprogram outdated data and eliminate distorted false truths that hold you prisoner from becoming an even better you. Discover and be your true self. Living your passion and purpose in life puts you in charge of your destiny. Your past story led to the present. Living in the present turns vision into reality. Operating outside your comfort zone creates your destiny as you perceive it."

Beverly Zeimet, Published Author, International Speaker, Identity Revelation Specialist, Vibrational Medicine Practitioner and Instructor, Retreat and Workshop Facilitator, Psychic, Emotional Healer and Spiritual Mentor.
BeverlyZ.Studio/BeverlyZeimet

My Journey

My Journey

"There are lots of programs out there that tell you how to write books fast and encourage you to produce quantity instead of quality. This is a list-building, sales-making mindset. It is true that having more products will gain you more attention. But if your books, courses, products are not quality offerings, all that attention quickly becomes negative. People spend their time on my ideas. I have to honor that. Quality wins EVERY time."

Toña Morales-Calkins, Writer, Publisher, Founder of Story Singer Media & Story-Singer-Media.com, Credentialed Teacher, Certified Business Trainer, Jewish Reverend, and multiple NaNoWriMo Winner.   Story-Singer-Media.com

My Journey

— <u>DAY 152</u> —

My Journey

"Time is a gift our modern anxious world denies. My life, once seemingly broken, existed in a fragmented state of depression, depletion and disease - and The GIFT came in the form of cancer to teach me, the healing gift of time.

Self-care is the antidote and the best preventative medicine that heals. You can learn how to re-condition your nervous system and overcome 'the anxiety experience' of life."

Wendy McMurdo, Author, Medical Intuitive, and Facilitator of Daily SLOW practices to help women navigate 'the anxiety experience' of life - so they can thrive.   Contented-Life.com.au

My Journey

_____

_____

_____

_____

_____

_____

_____

_____

_____

_____

_____

_____

_____

My Journey

"Stories tell the reality of the life we live. Stories tell the reality of life as we make it. Stories tell the decision to change the life we once knew. Stories, recrafted, tell the reality of life's new unfolding. Life's your story. Tell it like it is, in only the way you can. In story as in life, its characters are as outlandishly adventurous, deviously mischievous and outrageously zany as any of us truly are."

Grace Wolbrink, LMSW, Author and Storyteller, invites you to join her into the realm of story's vivid realism and adventurous unfolding.   Storyographers.com

My Journey

— _DAY 154_ —

My Journey

"*I was told I would be wasting my time writing a book because no one would be interested. But when I stood up at a networking group to speak and showed my first published book with my name as the author on the cover, I was asked to speak at two events. 'Courage to Live My Dream' provided me with speaking and teaching opportunities, and host of my own radio show. Follow your dream/heart desire.*"

La Wanna Parker, Author, Motivational Speaker, Radio Show Host, Creator of Emerging Personal Development Program, Companion for senior citizens, and Assistant with Project P.I.N.   LaWannaSpeaks.com

My Journey

My Journey

— *DAY 156* —

"The first time I looked into my son's eyes, I knew our destiny together was forged in love and that our journey would be on the road less travelled. His early years were shrouded in a deafening silence but relentlessly we dismantled the barriers and deconstructed the puzzle. My belief in him, my advanced soul, was as unwavering as my incessant faith. I trusted in God's Divine plans to deliver a miracle unto us — and so it was!"

"The Aussie Angel Lady," **Michelle Newten** assists people to connect with their Angels so that they can lead a more prosperous and easier life.   MichelleNewten.com

My Journey

My Journey

*"As humans, we desire to be successful and our lives become '**a journey-go-round**' like the merry-go-round ride we had fun riding as a kid. As a Visionarypreneur, I identified a $6 million opportunity and welcomed a team of four to embark on the journey with me to win the contract – and we did!*

The Journey-Go-Round in our adult lives is not always fun but we can make it fun by celebrating our wins. Enjoy the ride!"

Desheen L. Evans, Visionarypreneur, Executive/ Trauma Recovery Coach, Senior-level Trainer, is energized by connecting women to opportunities that promote professional revenue growth – the driving force to her success. <u>EyesofPower.com</u>

My Journey

— _DAY 157_ —

My Journey

"Without personal growth and development, I firmly believe we are moving backwards in life – not being a productive, contributing member of society. Every day we wake up with the opportunity to grow or drift; choose growth! Get out of your comfort zone! Coasting through life would not only cause me great regret at the end of this race, but also great sorrow. Today – grow, invest in you, and push yourself out of your comfort zone!"

Al (Allan) Ruttan is a Leadership Expert and an Executive Director with the John Maxwell Team. He is passionate about helping others reach their full potential. AlRuttan.com

My Journey

My Journey

"The easily traveled road is doubt and fear. It allows your creatively beautiful and powerful ideas to stagnate and rust. However, the Universe is doing all in its power to move us forward in the right direction. But we have to listen, believe, accept and receive. Let us refocus and expand our minds now. It is not easy but it is worth it. We must answer the door of opportunity. Let's see where it takes us!"

Ngiri Chavis, Certified Meditation Coach, has an expanding love for humanity. She puts people in touch with who they are. Together she helps energize and regenerate their lives.
nmcjgluv@gmail.com

My Journey

— _DAY 159_ —

My Journey

— _DAY 160_ —

"There are days you will want to quit. Days where everything just seems too hard. Stay the course. Those are the days where the magic happens.

Find people on the same journey as you and surround yourself in their love and support. I have an inner circle that supports my vision and they remind me why I'm on my journey. If you surrender to doubt and fear, you will miss the amazing transformation in store for you."

Christine Sterling, Business Success Coach, Award-Winning Romance Author and Creator of Where Women Write, supporting woman to write their first book.
ChristineSterling.com

My Journey

My Journey

"Some wisdom is gained from a constant checking in with yourself, your emotions, and your state of being. Check in to ask yourself the meaningful questions of 'what am I doing now,' 'why am I doing it,' 'what do I really want to be doing,' and 'does what I am doing have a purpose and make me feel good?' Hopefully, your answers – based in your own personal wisdom – will influence your actions positively."

Susan Schmidt, MLS, is a #1 International Best-Selling, Award-Winning Author, and a Research Consultant in the fields of complementary medicine, regenerative sciences and anti-aging technologies.   Susan@RegenerativeSciences.net

My Journey

— _DAY 161_ —

My Journey

"Success does not happen in a straight line. Success is more like a winding road. That's why the journey is more important than the destination. You're going to learn so much about yourself and your dreams, and your goals will naturally evolve to align with your growth. Smile for the journey and have confidence in your own strength to achieve the life you envision for yourself."

Audrey Hughey is the Founder of the Author Transformation Alliance, a tribe dedicated to uplifting and empowering authors to achieving their writing and publishing goals. TheWriteServices.com

My Journey

— _DAY 162_ —

My Journey

"I knew being paid monthly wasn't all that I desired; I wanted to discover who I am and impact lives. I admired others living their dreams and my change came when I decided to start with the little I knew and I grew daily. Learning from mentors placed me on a smart and fast lane. Do as much as you can with what you know now, the higher you go, the clearer it becomes."

Goodness Ben is an online entrepreneur, Business Coach, Speaker, Amazon Best-Selling Author and Founder of Bonita Creativity.   GoodnessBenOnline@gmail.com

My Journey

_____

_____

_____

_____

_____

_____

_____

_____

_____

_____

_____

_____

_____

— _DAY 163_ —

My Journey

"Albert Einstein said, 'There are only two ways to live your life. One is as though nothing is a miracle. The other is as though everything is a miracle.'

One's journey is determined by purpose, people, planning, persistence and always passion. As you contemplate your life, be inspired, courageous, authentic, integral and enthusiastic to share your gifts with others. Live your best life. Life IS a miracle. Embrace and Enjoy Your Journey! "

Beth McBlain, Author, Editor, Promoter, Publicist with strong client orientation by formulating and executing marketing, communications, branding, public/media relations strategies, event planning, collateral materials, researching and inspiring people. Beth.McBlain@gmail.com

My Journey

— _DAY 164_ —

My Journey

"Treat yourself like you would your best friend. When you start hearing those negative voices in your head, respond to them like you would if your best friend were saying those things about herself. You would probably be compassionate, supportive and loving to her. Do the same for yourself. What would you say to your best friend? Say those same things to yourself. Learn to love yourself as you do others."

Dr. Melanie Dunlap, Natural Health Practitioner, Wellness Coach and Author, teaches women how to use herbs, energy and ceremony as part of their healing process. MelanieDunlap.com

My Journey

_____

_____

_____

_____

_____

_____

_____

_____

_____

_____

_____

_____

_____

_____

My Journey

"I hovered between life and death wondering if my life was worth anything. My Dad's Wisdom came to mind. He asked me to get a bowl of water and blue food dye. He told me to put a few drops into the water, then stir it. The water turned blue. Dad asked me to retrieve the original three blue drops. Of course, I couldn't.

Remember: Everyone you've inspired has part of you in them that can never be removed."

Deborah Weed is the author and illustrator of *Paisley and Her Last Quill,* an imaginative children's book about a porcupine in the fashion industry.   <u>SelfWorthInitiative.net</u>

My Journey

— _DAY 166_ —

My Journey

— *DAY 167* —

"When you awaken the awareness of your senses, you are getting to know the untapped intricate places inside yourself in a most intimate way. To be able to make clear choices and understand your needs in the moment takes awareness. It means moving through the years of over-stimulation, numbness, and habit into more presence and love. Becoming aware of your senses starts with your breath — where the healing nature of curiosity is born!"

Tziporah Kingsbury, Best-Selling Author, Founder of The Soulful Relating Institute and Creator of the Soulful Relating 7 -Step System.   SoulfulRelatingInstitute.com

My Journey

....

....

....

....

....

....

....

....

....

....

....

....

....

....

My Journey

"Our Life Journey, our greatest adventure is an inside job: traveling and searching deep within, exploring who we really are, why we are here and what we intend to do with this one precious life we have been given. There is no better way to find out than through writing, journaling – daily. It is a catalyst for our visions and dreams, cathartic experience, springboard for ideas, food for our soul and our best travel companion."

Elisabeth Balcarczyk, M.A., PCC, Founder of Body Mind Soul Coaching, Transformational Leadership Workshops & Retreats Leader and Author, based in Germany.
coach_E_Balcarczyk@yahoo.com

My Journey

— _DAY 168_ —

My Journey

"In your journey to success, there will be struggles, bumps, setbacks, lapses and personal beliefs along the way that hold you back. All of this can also physically break your body down. Your health strengthens your courage to clear out limiting beliefs and energy blocks. Focus on building and then maintaining your health through eating properly and exercising. Health brings many benefits, from tackling anything Life throws at you to enjoying success and happiness."

Imelda Babia is a Diet/Health Consultant, Speaker and Author of *Why Most Weight-loss Diets Fail: A True Guide to a Fit, Healthy and Wealthy Lifestyle.* imee@ImeldaBabia.com

My Journey

....

....

....

....

....

....

....

....

....

....

....

....

My Journey

"Growing up blind, I faced low societal expectations. Not wanting my blindness to be the center of my story, I rarely wrote or spoke about it publicly. I worried that people would focus on my lack of sight and ignore my abilities.

I've started telling my story of empowerment and triumph. I faced fears and overcame challenges. People relate. They see me as capable of things many sighted people won't even try.

Choose your story and your message!"

As a copywriter and PR professional, **Krista Giannak** helps business owners and experts get noticed. WiseWordsThatMatter.com

My Journey

— _DAY 170_ —

My Journey

— _DAY 171_ —

"Women, you are the embodiment of wellness! You represent everything that's creative goodness, higher thinking, love, influence, power, beauty and holism. You are every woman but modern day life has left you overstressed, overworked and craving escapism. Living in wellness is not merely what you do but it radiates through your speech, home, style, couture, your fantasy of life and your swagger in
the world!

Cheers to 'Living More Effectively, Strategically and Intentionally Happy.'"

Bernadette C. Broughton is a Wellness LifeStyle & Real Estate Professional, Speaker and Author
BernadetteBroughton@comcast.net

My Journey

My Journey

"How do we overcome our penchant for being too hard on ourselves when we fail? And we will fail...

Grace – it's the word that rallies me to rise out of the pit of self-inflicted bullying and to learn from my mistakes.

Whether your first draft or proposal was garbage, whether you could've made a much better impression on a potential network source, give yourself grace and then move on toward greatness."

Leah Lindeman is the debut historical fiction author of *Redeemed From the Ashes* and her newest release, *Wisps of Gold.*   LeahLindeman.com

My Journey

— <u>DAY 172</u> —

My Journey

"I didn't realize it but my life had been in slow motion free fall for a long time. Then I was diagnosed with cancer. In putting myself back together through natural healing, pain has been a patient teacher.

You may not realize it, but your greatest gifts have come from the deepest challenges that you've faced. Scars really do become marks of beauty. Transformation begins when we listen to our heart and follow our joy."

Danielle Brooks, PhD. is a Medicine Singer, Mystic Mentor, Teacher and Writer. She weaves sacred songs of Creation that heal, unite and empower.   <u>PureGraceLight.com</u>

My Journey

— _DAY 173_ —

My Journey

"The greatest lesson I've learned in life: Awareness is everything and once you become aware, there's no going back! This gift of knowing empowers us to achieve lasting change and to live the truth of who we really are.

The journey begins when we consciously choose to truly care for ourselves and put our dreams first. Releasing our spirits to experience more freedom, creativity, love and joy in our lives; inspiring others and ultimately changing the world."

Tina Rusnak, Author, Speaker, Business/Life Coach at Tina Rusnak Unlimited, LLC, helps her clients discover and use their unique, unlimited possibilities to shine and thrive. TinaRusnakUnlimited.com

My Journey

— _DAY 174_ —

My Journey

"I'm grateful for my life journey of increasing love and happiness. I'm even grateful for the heartaches, struggles, joys, triumphs, and failures along my journey.

I'm grateful to now know the magic power of love, especially self-love.

When you practice gratitude, learn how to love yourself, and begin to acknowledge yourself daily for your accomplishments, big and small, you create a foundation of self-love on which to build your happiness and heart's desires."

Tina Nies is a Love Superhero, Life Coach, and #1 Best-Selling Author.   BeHappierToday.com

My Journey

_____

_____

_____

_____

_____

_____

_____

_____

_____

_____

_____

_____

_____

My Journey

"LIFE: Precious. Short. Delicate. Messy. Mysterious. Complicated. Happiness. Helpful. No matter how you look at it, LIFE is something you should never take for granted. Each person is given the one-time-only speech at the beginning and told I'll see you at the finish line. Live each day as if there was no tomorrow for there may not be one. You'll never have regrets, and a hell of a story to always tell."

Bonnie Boucek is a Reverend, Creative, an International Best-Selling Author, and a Fibromyalgia and Chronic Pain Life Coach.   BonnieBoucek@gmail.com

My Journey

— _DAY 176_ —

My Journey

— *DAY 177* —

"Wonderfully Outrageous Wealth Mindset!
Consider using the following 3 (Cs) to banish doubt, guilt and fear.

1. CALL in Love (divine assistance) and CALL out Fear (negative thoughts).

2. CHOOSE – A positive belief about yourself or the situation and reinforce it daily through words and actions.

3. CREATE – A relationship with a Mentor to help you take your next step toward the life you're truly meant to live."

Corine Wofford, CEO, Certified Master Facilitator and Best-Selling Author, speaks globally on Negotiation and Leadership, mentoring corporate leaders and women entrepreneurs worldwide to Be the Difference. CorineWofford.com

My Journey

— *DAY 177* —

My Journey

"The best thing about writing is it doesn't have to be perfect. Just put your pen to the paper and begin. Write whatever comes to mind. Make it 'pretty' later. First drafts should be raw, gritty, and unfiltered. It takes many drafts to get it right, but you gotta just do it! Imagine the feeling you'll have when you see your finished product compared to where you started. Trust the process, and let that ink flow."

Lisa Antley is an Author and Poet, who lives in Tennessee with her two daughters. Writing is her superpower!
Lisa Antley.webs.com

My Journey

— _DAY 178_ —

My Journey

"Maintain or regain your peace of mind. This is necessary in getting to 'your next', whether small scale/steps or large. It is vital to your psychological, physical, sociological, and emotional wellbeing. Seize the moment(s) with a peace of mind! Your days will be better! You will go further!

Peace will be your portion, through Jesus, the Prince of Peace, utilizing discernment, wise counsel, prayer, worship, and or meditation. Keep your Peace! You've got this!!"

Toya Hamlett, "The Visibility Strategist", International, Multi #1 and Award-Winning Best-Selling Author, Consultant, Assistant, Creative Director, Graphics, Print Media, Apparel, Transcription, Editing, Voiceovers, Accessories. ToyaHamlett3@gmail.com

My Journey

My Journey

— *DAY 180* —

"Did you know that your brain HAS to answer questions? So ask POSITIVE questions. Instead of 'Why am I always struggling financially?' ask: 'How am I financially abundant, having more than enough?

Your brain will work 24/7 to bring that about. Then pay attention to intuitive hits, such as to read a certain book or talk to a specific person, or even go to the store at a certain time. Then watch the magic happen!"

Bob Ross, EMT-D, Medical Physicist, Author, Musician, US Congressional Award Recipient, Inventor of a Nobel Prize-Worthy Brain Technique for Success and for Spontaneous Healing of Cancer. TheHiddenSecretToSuccess.com

My Journey

— <u>DAY 180</u> —

My Journey

"I'm amazed at how much our perception of others and the decisions we make, are influenced by past experiences and events that define our values, beliefs, expectations and willingness to trust and accept.

As a result, we may decide to buy a product/service, or not, based on our perceptions and assumptions, often without logical reason. Our reality of the world is often distorted, and we tend to perceive only those things which fit our beliefs."

Rod Adkins is a Business Executive based in Melbourne, Australia and a #1 International Best-Selling Author.
Rod@ActionMind.com.au

My Journey

— _DAY 181_ —

My Journey

— _DAY 182_ —

"Does a healthy person need to call 911? No. Only those in need of medical attention. Although that is a metaphor, in actuality, it's the truth. Most of mankind is in danger of losing their 'life.' Their REAL LIFE. Their souls. For all eternity. 'Call 911.' Believe in Jesus. He wants all of mankind to see the kingdom of God. Learn what is in the book of revelation. 'Call 911' TODAY!"

Dina M. Jones, Author of *Beheaded: The book of Revelation made simple with commentary*, CMD of Not Your Average Christian Ministry, and graduate of Theology at Princeton Theological Seminary.   https://www.facebook.com/nyaclife/

My Journey

— <u>*DAY 182*</u> —

My Journey

"At some point in life, everyone asks. What is my purpose, what are my tasks?

My journey here, is to understand. Who I AM...to learn firsthand.

The pains and sorrows, the joy and love. The lessons learned, to be part of...

Something good, and something grand. To share my gifts, and lend a hand.

To find my pieces, and mend my soul. Heal my spirit...that is the goal."

Kelly Dreisinger: Finding her voice through her poems, has given Kelly a purpose and a passion for inspiring others on their own journey.   Instagram: SoberAngel_Poet

My Journey

....

....

....

....

....

....

....

....

....

....

....

....

....

— _DAY 183_ —

My Journey

— *DAY 184* —

"They told her, life would never be easy - there were no more options. We refused their message and prescription for struggle and limitation, knowing deeply they were wrong about severe social anxiety. We turned over one thousand stones to eventually find an easy alternative buried in dismissed 1960's medical research.

Never settle for status quo! Dare to challenge when you know something is wrong or limited so you may discover your buried treasure!"

Jenna & Debbie VanderWeyden, Founders of Jenna and her Mom LLC, teach people how to shed social anxiety to live easy and comfortable in any situation. JennaAndHerMom.com

My Journey

— _DAY 184_ —

My Journey

— _DAY 185_ —

"You may not believe it, trust it, understand it, or even recognize it, but deep inside you can feel it! Your life has a heroic mission: a unique, powerful soul purpose that you alone were born to bring into glorious expression. The question is not whether each of us has a unique creative genius; the only question is whether each of us will have the faith, the courage, and the commitment to share it."

Sandra Cavanaugh, Creativity Specialist, Educator, and Writer/Director, coaches people of all ages and abilities to unleash their own unique creative genius with miraculous results. SandraCavanaugh.com

My Journey

....

....

....

....

....

....

....

....

....

....

....

....

....

— _DAY 185_ —

My Journey

"When you make the right choices in today's changing world, you will open the door to success. The key to success is often times locked away within you, your environment, your home and the people you are in contact with on a daily basis. If these things are contaminated with negative energy, you will need to decide on making changes which will be beneficial to your success."

Desziree Richardson is an experienced Broadcaster, International Best-Selling Award-Winning Author and the Founder of Women of Heart Foundation and Women of Heart Awards.   Desziree.com

My Journey

_____

_____

_____

_____

_____

_____

_____

_____

_____

_____

_____

_____

_____

_____

My Journey

"On my life's journey, I've come to the re-alization that we are all different threads in this great tapestry called Humanity. Most of us are committed to weaving beautiful   imagery with our strands - love, compassion, mercy. But others offer no more than a knotted, gnarly ugliness - racism, hatred, intolerance. This compels me to try even harder, love even deeper, and do more to soften my footsteps. Re-double your efforts - become the change."

Paige Speers has a BA in Dance. She lives in Missouri, is a creative type with interests in animals, nature and all arts.
RoxyJade83@gmail.com

My Journey

— _DAY 187_ —

My Journey

"You can manifest anything that you heart and soul desires. You just need to be crystal clear on what you truly desire, be aligned with your goal and believe it will happen, you need to leave the how up to the Universe and you need to take inspired action.

You are worthy of living a happy, fulfilled and abundant life. It is your time so GO for IT!"

Patricia LeBlanc is an Award-Winning Author, Intuitive Energy Healer/Teacher, and Manifesting Expert and can assist you to create the life that you truly desire.
PatriciaLeBlancHealing.com

My Journey

_____

_____

_____

_____

_____

_____

_____

_____

_____

_____

_____

_____

_____

— _DAY 188_ —

My Journey

"Many times, on life's journey we follow the directions of others, sometimes to our detriment. Get to know or at the least have a vision of your destination in mind so that you head in the right direction.

During your journey, you will need to take stock at times and make sure you are on the right path and that you still want the same destination.

Above all, enjoy your journey."

Shona Battersby – Spiritual Healing & Transformational Guidance using Reiki, Massage, Crystals and other tools.
ShonaBattersby@littlebearmedicine.co.business

My Journey

My Journey

"Your words become your reality.

When you think about something, but even more when you write it down, you take the first step towards materializing it. If all you're talking about is that life is too hard or that you can't succeed, then you'll probably be right.

Everyone can make excuses, but if you choose to always move forward and to focus on the positive in your life, then you'll start your journey towards success."

Catherine Lefebvre-Babinsky, Productivity Expert, Professional Problem Solver, Reformed Procrastinator, Book Fanatic and Founder of The Clever Achiever: helping business owners to boost their productivity. TheCleverAchiever.com

My Journey

_____

_____

_____

_____

_____

_____

_____

_____

_____

_____

_____

_____

_____

_____

— _DAY 190_ —

My Journey

"Less Stress, More Love on Your Emotional Intelligence Journey. We store trauma from personal events and global dramas. Unresolved stress disrupts sleep, energy and intimacy. Breakthrough Emotional Intelligence skills enhance our bodies', minds' and spirits' journeys through Relaxation - Empowerment - Passion - Renewal - Transformation.

We all feel emotional wounds. Self-awareness and truth are primary tools of intentional recovery. Trust your feelings and intuition. Write your wrongs. Bravely heal step-by-step. I teach verifiable techniques, transforming confident recovery into love."

Lance Ware, M.A., CHT, Heart and Soul Associates CEO; Stress Resolution and Trauma Recovery Certified Practitioner; Emotional Intelligence Trainer/Certification Provider; Editor; and Author of upcoming Emotional Intelligence book. LanceDouglasWare.com

My Journey

My Journey

"We are seasoned travelers of the labyrinth on our life's soul journey. On the beaten path and the road less traveled, the thirst for external fulfillment seems endless. Our inward journey, coming home to our true self, is most profound. We discover our wholeness and find ultimate fulfillment. Living well and loving well bring joy and contentment to our lives."

Dr. Jean Farish, Founder and CEO of "Life Care Wellness PEP For Angels, Inc., is a Life Care Coach and Award-Winning Author.   JeanFarishJourney.com

My Journey

_____

_____

_____

_____

_____

_____

_____

_____

_____

_____

_____

_____

_____

_____

_____

My Journey

"My heart was breaking watching people living lives of quiet desperation, not aligned with their purpose or dreams. I committed to live a life of total freedom and joy, regardless of circumstance and to ignite this in others. I found that limiting beliefs, decisions of defeat aren't as powerful as my Real Authentic Self. When you connect, nurture and source your life and decisions from YOU, magic happens. The world needs your gifts. Give them Now!"

Linda Robinson, Seminar Leader, Speaker, Transformational Success Coach, lives a life filled with passion, purpose, love, joy and success, and ignites that in her clients.
AwakeningToTruth.com

My Journey

— _DAY 193_ —

My Journey

— *DAY 194* —

"The life journey is the art of dancing with every experience, flowing with it, learning new steps on the way while finding your own rhythm and unique dance to share in love and joy. Staying true to you, trusting your intuitive guidance and keeping your energy clean will ensure an enjoyable journey. When you engage in the present moment with a clear mind and calm heart, you access your power to grow through every experience."

Martine Negro is Author of *Hacking the Well-Being Code* and her passion and expertise is restoring your energetic health so you can fully enjoy your life's journey.
MartineNegro.com

My Journey

— _DAY 194_ —

My Journey

— DAY 195 —

"It is your mindset that launches you into greatness. When you discipline your mind, control your thoughts, and be present in your thinking, you take back your power and really step into your future. Realize the power you have; you control you! You will manifest abundance in your life. What holds you back? Write some affirmations that put you in the driver's seat of your destiny. Change how you think, change your life."

Kimberly Anderson is an Intuitive Transformational Coach, Author, Motivational Speaker, and Mindset Mentor. Founder and Owner of InnerDimensional Healing.
KimberlyCAnderson.com

My Journey

My Journey

"The path to love, self-love and highest love is multi-dimensional. Through inquiry, space, breath and sound one can vibrate to touch oneness and live in one's body beyond limits. Mental and physical limitations surrendered to love produces a 'spiritual you'. The product of you is equal to the production of your thoughts and beliefs. Think and act in accordance to produce your highest self. Balance is key."

Tamee Knox, is a #1 International Best-Selling Author.
Shekhinahpath.com

My Journey

— *DAY 196* —

My Journey

"Experiencing a major pain, breakthrough or loss? Well, without the proper perspective, you will feel broken, ashamed, and even discouraged. However, one should not despair! There is still a bright light at the end of the tunnel. It's about changing your perspective on the matter to get you to the best version of yourself. Every experience in life is not a road block but a stepping stone to a more resilient YOU!"

Fayola Delica is a Passion and Purpose Activator, Minister, Registered Nurse, Entrepreneur, Award-Winning International Speaker, Author of 6 books, Beauty Queen, and Community Leader.   FayolaDelica.com

My Journey

— _DAY 197_ —

My Journey

— _DAY 198_ —

"I use to think that I needed someone else's expertise to help me heal. So much so that collectively over the years, I spent a fortune on experts guaranteeing my healing.

Through my journey, I have realized the day I stopped reaching out was the day I began to heal. The wisdom of understanding came from within knowing everything I needed to heal, I always had."

Nanci Stone, Author of *Kissing The Ground, A Personal Journey overcoming life's challenges using The Law of Attraction*, assists others in self-healing.
NStonecsi@gmail.com

My Journey

— _DAY 198_ —

My Journey

— *DAY 199* —

"I remember days recovering from an autoimmune condition and was bedridden.

The battle to reprogram my body was INTENSE.

I realized the biggest lessons are learned in crisis and can be our greatest catalyst for true change.

So, whatever obstacle you feel is in the way, it is actually the way towards FREEDOM!"

Susana Tuya Sarmiento, TV Presenter, Celebrity Speaker & 5-6 figures per month Online Mentor & Lifestyle Entrepreneur.   Susana.life

My Journey

My Journey

— *DAY 200* —

"My dogs were my dearest friends, my travel buddies, my soulmates. Our journeys were the stuff of dreams, and when they left, I believed my best life was behind me. The hardest journey I face now is one without them, but I'm never truly without them... my heart remembers, and so they live. If you feel lost and alone, let your heart remember. Your love still lives, and it's always near you on your journey."

Gina Longo, former airline captain, solo traveler (with her German Shepherds), and the creator and author of *Britain Unleashed*—dog-friendly historical travel stories with a cheeky twist.   BritainUnleashed.com

My Journey

— _DAY 200_ —

My Journey

"Are you where you want to be in life? If not, a Life Coach can be helpful. An independent and professional coach will work with you to determine what's important to <u>you</u>, then both support and challenge you to break down the barriers and limitations that stand in your way. Be the priority in your own life, find a Life Coach with whom you can be honest, and be brave, live the life you desire."

Michelle Everingham, GradDip Psych, B.Bus Bus Mgt/Psych, qualified Life Coach, Mentor, and #1 International Best-Selling Author, inspires and supports women achieve their personal, spiritual and professional potential.
MichelleEveringham.com

My Journey

My Journey

"Unexpected things happen in life and throw us off guard and are completely out of our control.

We may not have the control over the situation but we do have a choice in our reaction and meaning we give to it.

You can give a very dis-empowering meaning to something and become very stuck or give an empowering meaning and move forward. For example, 'This is stressful' to 'This is exciting or a new challenge.'"

Liza Sager, Mother of 5, Certified Life Coach, Strategic Interventionist, and Survivor of domestic abuse. YOU are the change you need. facebook.com/InspiringYouToShine/

My Journey

My Journey

"As a Business Owner, do you spend too much time working 'in' your business, and not enough time working 'on' your business? Do you feel frustrated and disillusioned with your business? What to do? Sometimes a new vision does the trick or an updated mission statement or new goals. Maybe the best solution is to hire a team that work with you in rejuvenating your enthusiasm for your business."

Connie Petcu helps overworked Business Owners to clarify and prioritize their focus, so that they can make more money, while working a lot less.   Kf4jsa@gmail.com

My Journey

— <u>DAY 203</u> —

My Journey

— *DAY 204* —

"It's important to realize that the past does not define you! When voices of "You're not good enough!" and all the other "You're not" come rushing in, know that these are limiting beliefs. When you feel like life is holding you down or trying to count you out, know that you are on the path to greatness and deserve to learn how to release this and live the life you love and deserve!"

Elise Perry is a Divine Wellness Coach helping people live healthy, happy lives using natural approaches so they're excited to wake up and love life!   <u>EliseAPerry.com</u>

My Journey

— _DAY 204_ —

My Journey

" 'What do you want to be when you grow up?' can be a daunting question! My own 'career confusion' eventually led me down a path to help others find clarity regarding their career or life purpose. Perhaps your journey is a similar one. What do you love to do? What is your passion? Chances are following that passion can lead you to your life purpose."

Carmen Croonquist, Founder of Intentionality Coaching & Consulting Services, merges positive psychology with power coaching to help individuals create a "life by design." bit.ly/CarmenCroonquist.com

My Journey

My Journey

"You are powerful and resilient! Remember this when feeling stuck in the midst of chaos and adversity. Know there is always hope! You can find your way and rise above! Go within to your heart-space; feel yourself wrapped in the essence of divine love. Discover your calm, peaceful center and tap into your innate resources. Draw on your inner strength to help carry you through. Your power and answers always lie within you!"

Annette Meinzer is a Transpersonal Coach guiding those experiencing a sense of loss on a journey of discovering self, inner peace and joy in life.   DiscoveringNewLife.com

My Journey

— _DAY 206_ —

My Journey

"Deep down you already know who you are. That small voice in the back of your mind has been whispering to you since your beginning. What if you really listened, explored, and allowed your heart, mind, and body to connect to your Authentic Self? Your purpose would become clear, and what you discover about yourself could pave the way as you step into each new season of your life."

Monique Brinkman-Hill is a Transformative Coach who empowers women to live their most authentic life and unleash their unique power and purpose through every season of their lives.   MBHCoachingandConsulting.com

My Journey

— _DAY 207_ —

My Journey

"No matter if you are a healer or not, you can suffer from burnout, which will extinguish your light, energy and passion! The healing prescription is simple but critical and can save your life. All you have to do is give yourself permission to say 'yes' to daily self-care for yourself. Self-care ignites the body, soul and spirit's ability to start each day recharged and illuminated to help those we encounter who are in need."

Dr. Davia Coutcher D.D. S.C. provides wholistic care for established professionals. Her practice empowers and assists those who help the masses to take of themselves first. SimplyDavia@gmail.com

My Journey

— _DAY 208_ —

My Journey

— *DAY 209* —

"How do you know the things that you do?" is the common phrase that I am asked on a daily basis. I tell them that if you listen carefully, you can hear God speaking to you. God gives each person spiritual gifts to lead and guide others. God gifted me with knowledge that a normal person would not know. Use your gift to lead and light up the world."

Dahlia Ashford, Life Coach, Independent Educational Consultant, and Founder of Transform. Evolve. Transcend., LLC.   TransformETranscendLLC@gmail.com

My Journey

— _DAY 209_ —

My Journey

"Have you ever wanted to see an end to pain and suffering in the world? Through my own profoundly transformational experiences accessing higher states of consciousness and my own major life changes, I saw this was possible and that every illness and emotional challenge can be healed. You are walking magic and can find your inner wand. With the help of your Higher Self, you can eliminate any challenge – major or minor – that you are facing."

Karin Eke, Lightworker, Mystic, Energy Healer, Empath, is passionate about infinite human potential, the magic of life, and helps people connect deeply with their Higher Self. TheAscensionPath.com

My Journey

My Journey

"Forgive? Are you kidding me? With what I've been through?

Yes, I too have been through sexual abuse, mental and emotional abuse, three disappointing marriages and three divorces, stage IV throat cancer, and more.

Like a cancer, bitterness eats away at us.

Forgiveness doesn't condone abusive behaviour but it frees us of the pain and torment and gives us the freedom to live in victory. Recognize the need and then be willing is the first step."

An inspirational, dynamic Speaker and Coach, **Irene Bryant**, works with people who want to experience freedom from resentment through forgiveness so they live in victory. IreneBryant.com

My Journey

— _DAY 211_ —

My Journey

*"This is my cure for self-doubt, a way to silence that voice that keeps me stuck: I recall the gurus, writers, artists, who inspired and guided me, and I ask, "Who would I be, what would my life be like, if **they** had doubted their abilities, if **they** hadn't taken that first step, if **they** hadn't failed and tried again?" And with deep gratitude for all those who have gone before me, I take action."*

Pamela Driscoll - Goddess With a Day Job - is a Transformational Coach helping women tap into their inner wisdom/ divine power to live with clarity, joy, and courage.
facebook.com/CoachingWithPam

My Journey

— _DAY 212_ —

My Journey

"Have you set a goal only to be disappointed? When you're attached to an outcome, you're trying to bend the Universe to your will. That generally doesn't work. Goals are most effective when used to set your direction and choose your action steps.

With your direction set, focus on the steps. No one can control the outcome. You can control completing your action steps. This is the secret behind 'life is about the journey, not the destination'."

Joe Murphy, Entrepreneur, Navigator of Life and Transitioning Guide. He offers refreshing insights on life's challenges/rough spots on his website.   LivingFullTilt.com

My Journey

— _DAY 213_ —

My Journey

Afterword
By Dane Russo, Ph.D.

"**One Question**"

One question. One answer. That's all you get.

You have been granted the answer to any question you ask.

The outcome may very well affect the rest of your life. What would you ask?

My experience is that there is no one single question that people ask nor even a single question theme. Why is that?

We all have more in common than not. Chemically, we are all made of and shall end as star dust. We share a multitude of experiences, such as birth, death, marriage, divorce, sickness, education, work, laughs, tears, and doubts. We share with others knowledge and empathy. Yet despite this commonality, we all seek different answers.

So, I ask, what would be your question and why might you ask it? How could the answer affect your life?

Dane Russo received his Ph.D. in psychology from the University of Texas.

Dane worked for 38 years in the Human Health and Performance Directorate at NASA's Johnson Space Center in Houston, Texas.

During his career at NASA, Dane worked in Medical Operations, the Biomedical Laboratories Branch, and the Human Systems Engineering and Development Division.

He served as Branch Chief for multiple branches, as the Advanced Human Support Technology Program Manager, as the Space Human Factors and Habitability Element Manager, and as an Assistant Division Chief.

He now lives with his wife, Jean in Manzanillo, Mexico.

Connect with Dane at: bbcards46@hotmail.com

— Index —

— Index —

– Index –

ALSO FROM EXPERT INSIGHTS PUBLISHING

#1 International Best-Selling Books:

100 Top Tips for Writers
Are YOU the Missing Piece? Journal
Become a Bestseller and PR Magnet
Beyond Your Book
Birthing Your Book
Cancer: From Tears to Triumph
My Big Idea Book
My Big Idea Workbook
My Creative Ideas Journal
Ready, Aim, Captivate!
Ready, Aim, Excel!
Ready, Aim, Impact!
Ready, Aim, Influence!
Ready, Aim, Inspire!
Ready, Aim, Soar!
Ready, Aim, Thrive!
Tail Waggin' Tales
Wounded? Survive! Thrive!!!

Award-Winning Magazines:

Insights Magazine
PUBLISHED! Magazine
Stress Free Magazine
Resources Uncovered Magazine

About Expert Insights Publishing

Our mission is to give authors a voice and a platform on which to stand. We specialize in books covering innovative ways to meet the personal and business challenges of the 21st century.

Through our signature, inexpensive publishing and marketing services, we help authors publish and promote their works more effectively and connect to readers in a uniquely efficient system.

We employ an experienced team of online marketing strategists, ad copywriters, graphic artists, and Web designers whose combined talents ensure beautiful books, effective online marketing campaigns at easily affordable rates, and personal attention to you and your needs.

We have promoted over 1,200 authors to bestseller status. Will YOU be next?

Learn more about our current publishing opportunities at:

ExpertInsightsPublishing.com

Made in the USA
San Bernardino, CA
30 November 2018